Organization and Management in CHINA 1979–1990

International Studies In Management and Organization:
A Companion Book Series
Jean Boddewyn, Series Editor

ORGANIZATION AND MANAGEMENT IN CHINA, 1979–1990
Edited by Oded Shenkar

Organization and Management in CHINA 1979–1990

Oded Shenkar, Editor

M. E. Sharpe, Inc.
Armonk, New York • London, England

Available in the United Kingdom and Europe from M. E. Sharpe, Publishers,
3 Henrietta Street, London WC2E 8LU.

Previously published as Volume 20, Number 1–2 of *Organization and Management in
China 1979–1990*.

Library of Congress Cataloging-in-Publication Data

Organization and management in China, 1979–1990 / edited by Oded Shenkar.
    p. cm.
    Includes bibliographical references and index.
    ISBN 0-87332-818-3
    1. Industrial management—China. 2. Industrial organization—China.
  I. Shenkar, Oded.
HD70.C5074   1991
658′.0095′09048—dc20   91-6387
                                    CIP

Printed in the United States of America.

⊖

HA   10 9 8 7 6 5 4 3 2 1

To my father

Contents

Introduction

For over a decade now, the People's Republic of China (PRC) has been engaged in one of the most comprehensive management reforms ever undertaken. The success—or failure—of these reforms carries far-reaching implications. For China, these reforms will most likely determine its ability to modernize and become a major power in the world economy. At the same time, the reforms touch on major political and social issues within the PRC, therefore affecting the structure and control of Chinese society. And while China's economic modernization is of interest to its major trade partners, as well as low-cost competitors, its political and social transformation is equally important to Hong Kong (which reverts back to Chinese rule in 1997) and to Taiwan (which shares the reunification goal with the People's Republic). For the Soviet Union and some Eastern bloc countries, China represents a model for introducing limited market mechanisms into a centrally planned economy while rejecting full-fledged capitalism and some of its political correlates. Finally, the scale and nature of the PRC reforms make them indispensable to management theorists and practitioners with interests ranging from comparative management to organizational change.

The Chinese reforms—to the extent that they have not been rolled back—take place within a difficult business environment, whose major stakeholders are not always supportive of (and are sometimes outright hostile to) such reforms. Among such hostile stakeholders are party officials, who see their ideology threatened and their authority eroding, and senior state bureaucrats, who are hard-pressed to yield decision-making power to lower administrative levels and to the enterprise management. Other dissatisfied elements include employees and managers who cannot adjust to a competitive, performance-based system, and residents of poorer provinces who are increasingly bitter about the relative riches of the coastal provinces and Special Economic Zones (SEZs).

It is impossible to determine to what extent such disenchantment contributed to the events culminating in the Tiananmen massacre, but it is safe to assume that it did play a prominent role. In any event, the massacre and the subsequent conservative backlash are already affecting the management reforms in a number of ways. The attempt to curb the number and scale of collective and private enterprises punishes those organizations that have been the boldest in introducing organizational reforms such as performance-based pay. The renewed emphasis on party control robs Chinese managers from the limited measure of control they acquired over the last decade. The new limits on PRC students allowed to study abroad (particularly in the United States) deprive Chinese enterprises of potential change agents who could apply their foreign-acquired skills to those firms.

The present colledtion provides an analysis of Chinese management and organizations at this crucial juncture. The first seven chapters assess the impact of the reforms on domestic Chinese enterprises across such diverse issues as decision making, work values, and managerial behavior. These are followed by three chapters on foreign joint ventures, and three chapters on trade and trade organizations. Together, these chapters give the reader a snapshot of management in the PRC prior to 1989 as well as a preliminary judgment on possible changes in the near future.

Over the last few years we have heard repeatedly that China has reached "a point of no return" in its reform program, and that a return to the "old ways" was inconceivable. While a 180 degree return is not yet in sight, it is already clear that the legacy of a centrally planned economy and of dual party–state control has not been entirely erased by a decade of reforms, no matter how extensive and success-ful. Schermerhorn's and Nyaw's article reminds us how important this legacy is. "The past," they suggest, "holds too great a grasp on the present and future," a statement that now seems even more relevant. The authors propose that "learned helplessness" is one of the main legacies of the PRC tradition, the result of state and party interference in every aspect of the enterprise life. The reforms were expected to alter that strict control, but so far they could only make some serious dents in it. Among other factors, this failure is enhanced by a very long tradition of bureaucratic economy. For thousands of years, the Chinese imperial bureau-cracy regulated virtually all economic activity in China, leaving very little room for individual entrepreneurship and the development of autonomous organiza-tional units. It was against this background, as well as Marxist dictates, that the People's Republic centrally planned economy was established. To ensure a uni-fied, centralized, and highly controlled nation, it was also deemed necessary to ensure the grip of the party and state apparati on the business enterprise.

To enable limited enterprise autonomy without loosening central control, the Chinese leadership under Deng Xiaoping orchestrated a shift toward "market socialism," a hybrid of central planning and limited market mechanisms. In reality, Wang, Wang, and Gong report, diverse markets have developed with variations existing along regional and ownership lines. Operating within a dual structure of a planning sector on one hand, and a quasi-free exchange on the other hand, has proven to be a major headache for both planners and managers who have to make decisions under such adverse conditions.

Generations of tight planning and an oscillating policy line have produced a manager who is frequently incapable of or unwilling to accept responsibility, even when such responsibility is being delegated, and is hardly accustomed to making actual decisions. Creating such decision capability was and remains crucial to the reform effort. Fischer, Blackmon, and Woodward examine that crucial aspect of decison making as it relates to project selections made by PRC managers. While affirming the central planning legacy, the study identified significant changes in decision processes that were taking place at the time the survey was taken (1983/84). Whether those changes are indicative of the decision-making processes of Chinese managers today is not known; however, because the organizations involved were at the forefront of reform, the study may be an accurate representation of more recent processes in regular firms.

Graf, Hemmasi, Lust, and Liang also examine managers who are at the forefront of China's development. They surveyed research managers regarding actual and desirable organizational characteristics, and found a desire for more participative management, more frequent feed-back, and performance-based pay. However, these managers also expressed a need for greater reliance on formal plans and uniform guidelines, a reflection, perhaps, of the legacy of a planned economy, combined with inability to handle a growing environmental diversity. This latter desire can also be explained by a feeling that PRC managers lack the skills necessary for effective decision making. Indeed, Stewart and Chong reported that personal training and development were perceived as crucial factors for career success by senior PRC managers.

The managers in the Stewart and Chong study had no formal business education, which is quite typical of the older generation of PRC managers. It is thus important to examine the attitudes of the future managers who will have to bear the burden of reform. This is what Specter and Solomon have done, in a comparative study of attitudes and motivations among Chinese business students in Shanghai and two samples of U.S. business students. They found that U.S. students in both Miami and Baltimore scored higher than their PRC counterparts on four traits linked to managerial success, but cautioned about the relevance of those traits in the Chinese environment. However, this environment continues to evolve, and with it the success traits may change as well.

Minor and Hamm look at the Newly Industrialized Countries (NICs) as possible role models for China. The authors review development models which could be applicable to the PRC experience, and outline some of their managerial applications. Yet, once more China might chart its own individual course, seeking its own solutions to its problems.

Such problems are abundant. Threatened by spiralling inflation, renewed factionalism, growing disenchantment of various segments of the population, and, more recently, social and political upheaval, the PRC leadership decided to put the brakes on its decade-old economic reforms. While organizational reforms have not been labeled a direct target of the present conservative backlash, it is already apparent that at the very least the reforms have been temporarily halted. The question now is for how long (senior Chinese sources suggest three years) and to what extent the current reforms might be rolled back.

The organizational reforms are especially fragile because of the stage in which they have been halted. China is now in the midst of transition. It is still managed by a centrally planned, bureaucratic system, but already has in place quite a few elements of the so-called "market socialism." Needless to say, both systems have advantages and disadvantages, but there are special perils associated with the fact that the Chinese economy is at present neither here nor there. There are special management problems associated with the state of transition. For instance, one of the major reforms in the compensation system of Chinese enterprises has been to tie executive and employee remuneration to enterprise profitability. The problem is that, until price reforms are introduced, enterprise profitability cannot seriously be considered as a measure of a manager's qualifications or hard work. The much touted autonomy of enterprise directors is another example. As long as raw materials and products are centrally allocated, managers have very little leeway in making the important decisions in the enterprise. In both instances, the reforms have created considerable expectations that have not been fulfilled.

Many of those expectations have been formed in relation to foreign entities becoming major players in the Chinese economy as both traders and manufacturers. The launch of China's reform drive in 1978 signaled a new era in trade and foreign direct investment (FDI). To gain the foreign currency and technological know-how so vital to its modernization, the Chinese leadership decided to open up the country in an uprecedented manner. The volume of foreign trade grew rapidly, with the United States, Europe, and Japan becoming major trade partners. More importantly, after a quarter of a century during which FDI was all but suspended, China embarked on a major drive to solicit investment from Developed and Newly Industrialized Countries (NICs). This drive has culminated in the Joint Venture Law of 1979, which set the framework for establishing foreign–PRC joint enterprises.

The Chinese leadership saw foreign joint ventures as the most effective vehicle for realizing some of its crucial objectives: to gain technology transfer, to generate foreign exchange, to enhance reputation and market recognition for Chinese products, to allow PRC enterprises to learn valuable management skills, and to mobilize the capital necessary for rapid modernization. The many problems that arose in the management of these enterprises should not distract attention from the relative success the Chinese have had with realizing at least some of their set objectives.

Teagarden and Von Glinow propose a typology of Sino–foreign alliances based on two dimensions: (1) obligation, namely the profit allocation structure, rights, and obligations, and (2) involvement, namely, the degree of partner interdependence. This typology provides a useful framework for analyzing the current population of alliances and foreign joint ventures in China and their operational problems. In particular, the interdependence of the Chinese and foreign parent companies has important implications for the management hurdles that are likely to arise in such joint ventures, as well as for the environmental changes they face. Such interpedendence becomes crucial when ventures need to operate in a less hospitable business climate, as is the case today.

Managing a foreign joint venture is complex in any country, and China is no exception (to say the least). One reason for this complexity is the existence of a great variety of stakeholders, many of whom are not familiar to the foreign parent. Nyaw studies a major stakeholder in international joint ventures in China whose role has not been explored so far—the trade union. He emphasizes that the role played by unions in foreign joint ventures differs significantly from their role in domestic PRC enterprises, and has much to do with interlocking the ventures with various party and state agencies. With the party and state now assuming broader responsibilities, these interlocking functions may become even more important.

Even before foreign joint ventures are formed, prospective parents formulate expectations regarding their ideal mode of operation—expectations that later tend to coincide or conflict, with major repercussions to the ventures. Baird, Lyles, Ji, and Wharton studied the attitudinal differences between U.S. and PRC managers in regard to the management of foreign joint ventures. They found several key differences in preferences toward organizational structure, employment patterns, work norms, and compensation systems. It is worthwhile to remember, of course, that such attitudinal differences are common to international joint ventures worldwide, although they tend to be accentuated in China because of the sharp cultural, legal, and organizational differences between the Chinese environment and the environment of many foreign parents.

The last three articles in this volume are all concerned with foreign trade involving PRC organizations. Frankenstein examines changes in the Chinese trade environment, emphasizing the transitional nature of the current business climate, and the persistence of "politics in command," even during the reform period. Needless to say, we have all been reminded of that reality recently.

Punnett and Yu remind us of the key role played by the foreign partner in trade transactions. They compare the attitudes of Canadian and U.S. companies toward doing business with the PRC, and identify a number of significant differences in their perceptions of the Chinese market. Some of these differences, however, may be related to the different sizes of U.S. and Canadian firms in the survey.

Finally, Vernon-Wortzel, Wortzel, and Zhu investigate the PRC side of trade, namely how Chinese organizations confront the export challenge. They suggest that in the face of increased competition from low-cost producers, Chinese firms will have to increase productivity substantially. The need to be competitive will expose PRC firms to a pressure toward increased productivity. Export success will in turn bring in the foreign currency so essential to the purchase of machinery and technological know-how.

It is impossible to conclude this volume without referring again to the recent events of spring 1989, events that are now more glaring in light of the recent developments in Eastern Europe. For a generation of Chinese managers and employees who in their lifetime have already seen several ups and downs, the conservative backlash is most alarming. Reports of the party attempting to reassert its control at various organizational levels suggest that the struggle over the future of Chinese management and organization is far from over. The outcome of that struggle has not been decided at this time. It is doubtful whether it will be resolved any time soon, but China can ill afford to wait. Hopes that foreign enterprises will lead the way are also fading. At this time, FDI has practically dried up, with many projects already in the pipeline suspended. Most foreign company executives we interviewed have adopted a "wait-and-see" approach. If the current atmosphere does not improve, the result will be a virtual halt in FDI as well as the shifting of production lines to other countries. Already, foreign firms find countries such as Thailand and Indonesia attractive alternatives that provide a skilled and low-cost labor as well as political stability. Suddenly, Eastern European nations have also become major pursuers of foreign investment capital. To remain competitive, China will have to offer better incentives and higher returns to foreign investors in order to compensate for a higher political risk level. Reassuring the foreign investor and trader with positive comments on continuous openness may not be sufficient at this point. A failure to follow such commitments with concrete steps will have serious consequences for the prospects of continuous growth and economic modernization.

Acknowledgment

Grateful acknowledgment is made to the Pacific Asian Management Institute at the College of Business Administration, University of Hawaii at Manoa for the generous support provided to this project.

ODED SHENKAR
Tel Aviv University
and University of Hawaii

PART ONE

DOMESTIC ENTERPRISES

JOHN R. SCHERMERHORN, JR.,
AND MEE-KAU NYAW

Managerial Leadership in Chinese Industrial Enterprises

Legacies of Complex Structures and Communist Party Involvement

The management literature is now replete with observations, commentary, and empirical research on continuing reforms of state-owned industrial enterprises in the People's Republic of China. The foundation work of Tung (1982) is complemented by an increasing number and variety of responsible contributions whose predominant concerns include management development (Warner, 1985), value comparisons (Lai and Lam, 1985; Shenkar and Ronen, 1987), structural arrangements (Warner and Nyaw, 1986), negotiating patterns and business style (Frankenstein, 1986), and broader political–economic perspectives (Bachman, 1988; Petras, 1988).

Among these books and articles, however, there is some inclination to focus attention on changes occurring in Chinese institutions as a result of recent reforms. This is the case even though Chinese society retains an underlying conservatism resulting in a pattern of "ups *and* downs" or "speed-ups *and* slow-downs" as it adjusts and readjusts on the political, economic, and business scenes (Henley and Nyaw, 1986b; Petras, 1988). The massacre in Beijing at Tiananmen Square on June 4, 1989, and subsequent reactionary treatment of student leaders and sympathizers of the "democracy" movement, are dramatic and most unfortunate cases-in-point.

Facing sanctions and criticisms from other nations of the world for its handling of this internal turmoil, China's communist leadership has had to reassess the country's economic reforms in the context of emerging sociopolitical developments. But even as another period of adjustment unfolds, the continuing strength and enduring influence of China's politically based institutions and in-

The authors are Charles G. O'Bleness Professor of Management at Ohio University, Athens, OH, and Chairman of the Department of Organization and Management, Chinese University of Hong Kong, respectively.

frastructure remains apparent. There is a need, accordingly, for organization theorists to give increased attention to the historical aspects of institutional change and political control as they affect the management of industrial enterprises in China. Schermerhorn (1987) identifies three paradoxes that deserve special consideration in this regard.

1. *The paradox of the enterprise operating environment.* Chinese industrial enterprises operate in a reform environment that seeks greater economic growth and offers new market freedoms, yet the enterprises are still influenced by central planning tendencies that constrain them.

2. *The paradox of the enterprise organization structure.* Chinese industrial enterprises face pressures to increase productivity and business performance, yet they must simultaneously support multiple systems that serve political and social objectives.

3. *The paradox of the enterprise power structure.* Factory directors and the management cadre in Chinese industrial enterprises are assuming greater responsibilities for performance results, but internal checks and balances in parallel authority structures remain strongly influenced by the Chinese Communist Party.

Paradoxes such as these have important implications for the emergence of managerial leadership in Chinese firms. Many (if not most) enterprises have struggled over the past several years to respond to "new" administrative initiatives encouraged under the reforms (Burton, 1987). But the pace of truly transformational change is hampered by an entrenched state bureaucracy with strong roots to the past (Henley and Nyaw, 1986a), the failure of many managers to assume authority commensurate with their performance responsibilities (Boisot and Child, 1988), and political risk tracing to the continued influence and self interests of the Chinese Communist Party (Bachman, 1988; Petras, 1988). As highlighted once again by the 1989 Tiananmen events, forty-plus years of socialism and a strong party presence in all aspects of Chinese society are proving to be conservative forces even in a reform environment.

At a minimum, therefore, what can be expected of this historical context for present-day action in Chinese enterprise is organizational change that will remain inherently incremental. The core nature of the contemporary Chinese sociopolitical milieu may constrain future developments to those which, as Cyert and March (1963) would suggest, fall "in the neighborhood" of past operations. Thus, the remainder of this paper examines the traditions established by complex enterprise structures and Communist Party involvement, with special interest in their implications for managerial leadership.

The complex organization of Chinese industrial enterprise

State-owned Chinese industrial enterprises, as described by Henley and Nyaw, 1986a), are structured quite differently from their typical Western counterparts.

Many of their characteristic features are byproducts of China's socialist environment, and they are quite enduring. Even as the reforms continue to evolve, the presence of simultaneous systems and parallel authority structures lend a unique "Chinese" character to any firm (Schermerhorn, 1987).

Simultaneous systems

Figure 1 portrays three systems that operate "simultaneously" to create the typical Chinese industrial enterprise: the life support, sociopolitical support, and business and operations systems. Of these, only the last is shared in common with most Western commercial enterprises. The other two systems are "ancillary" and have no direct relationship to the production of goods or services. They achieve meaning only in the broader setting of China's socialist society, which views all organizations as instruments of the state.

Components of the *enterprise life-support system* assist workers to fulfill such necessities of everyday life as housing, health care, child-care and education, and even recreation and entertainment. They involve the employing firm in assisting a worker's entire family in meeting their daily needs, and they represent a large proportion of any enterprise's day-to-day operating concerns (Ignatius, 1989b). The extent of this commitment is illustrated at the First Automobile Works in Changchun, where some 80 percent of 60,000 total workers are employed in ways totally unrelated to car production—everything from barbering to police work. The factory director is quoted as saying: "Each year, I have to worry about housing for 2,000 couples getting married, nurseries for 2,000 newborn babies, and jobs for 2,500 school-leavers. I am mayor as well as factory head. Of course I have a bigger burden than my counterparts in the U.S." (Leung, 1989: A14).

Components of the *enterprise sociopolitical support system*, by contrast, are designed to advance socialist ideology. To this extent, Redding and Wong (1986) consider Chinese organizations as "politically dominated" and designed in part with ideological purposes in mind. The enterprise branch of the Chinese Communist Party is the center point for this ideology. Sociopolitical support systems such as the following exist within the firm and allow the party to exert a "political" presence:

Worker's Union: An enterprise branch of a national trade union with the objective of advancing worker welfare within the firm.

Women's Federation: An enterprise unit with the primary objective of safeguarding female rights.

Communist Youth League: An enterprise branch of a national youth league with the primary objective of helping the party express itself to young workers and young members of workers' families.

Militia: An enterprise unit with the primary objective of creating a paramilitary self-defense capability among workers.

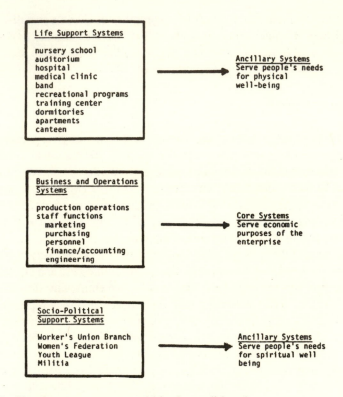

Figure 1. Simultaneous systems within the traditional
      Chinese industrial enterprise

Both the life-support and sociopolitical-support systems complicate the operating structures of Chinese organizations. They also extend managerial responsibilities into a far broader arena than is typical to most western organizations. The
"Chinese" firm is, therefore, quite distinctive in the internal complications that
result from its simultaneous systems.

Parallel authority structures

As shown in Figure 2, "administrative" and "party" authority co-exist within the
Chinese industrial enterprise. Although reforms have sought broader roles for
factory directors and administrative cadre, enterprise party secretaries and the
party cadre remain formally vested in the organization structure (Jiang, 1980;
Tung, 1982; Zhu, 1985; Henley and Nyaw, 1986a; Petras, 1988). Through its
presence in a "parallel" authority structure, the party reserves a potentially active
and influential role in most enterprise decisions.

The party's authority within the enterprise has traditionally led to involvement in matters of managerial *control*—making sure that the factory director and other administrators work according to state and party plans and policies, and managerial *motivation*—stepping in to encourage people to work hard on behalf of the socialist state. At the Xian Department Store, for example, a policy to identify publicly the "Forty Worst Shop Assistants" was initiated to correct poor customer service. The store's Communist Party secretary was quoted as saying (Ignatius, 1989a: 1): "It's the only system we've found to pressure workers to do better. Those designated the 'worst' feel embarrassed. Otherwise, our efforts would have no effect." A contrite salesclerk whose name appeared on the list was quoted as lamenting: "I accept my punishment. . . . I view my little three-foot shop counter as a window of socialist civilization."

In this and many other ways, Chinese institutions thus operate in the boundaries of the parallel authority structure depicted in Figure 2. Within any individual enterprise, it is not uncommon for the party cadre to be involved in appointing the factory director and other high-level officials at one decision-making extreme, and in making employee compensation and discipline decisions at the other. Furthermore, this party involvement stands in addition to its active role in such ancillary units as the enterprise workers union and workers congress (Henley and Nyaw, 1986a)—many high-ranking trade unionists and representatives of workers congresses are themselves party members. This means that the party's influence in each firm is very highly integrated. In many cases, it is the party structure that serves as final arbiter of disputes arising within or among the many disparate internal units of the enterprise (Henley and Nyaw, 1987). In all cases, the existence of party influence through the parallel authority structures complicates management and administrative processes in Chinese industrial enterprises.

Perspectives on the emergence of managerial leadership

China's management reform program since 1979 has pressured enterprise administrators to think strategically, to be business oriented rather than production oriented, to take greater risks, and to be more entrepreneurial (Ma, 1980; Kasper, 1982; Byrd and Tydrick, 1984). Yet, when viewed from the structural perspective just presented, it is clear that the emergence of new "managerial leadership" in Chinese firms is constrained by forces of contemporary history.

At a most fundamental level, the traditional management functions have each been to some extent accomplished in the past by persons or groups other than a firm's administrative officials. *Planning* was largely done according to the mandates of state plans and by local government and ministerial interpretations of these plans into enterprise objectives. *Organizing* was minimized, since the complex internal organization of simultaneous systems and parallel authority structures permeated and restricted the very essence of Chinese industrial enterprise. *Leading* was constrained by a lack of managerial authority singularly to direct worker performance as the party cadre often assumed dominant roles in "encour-

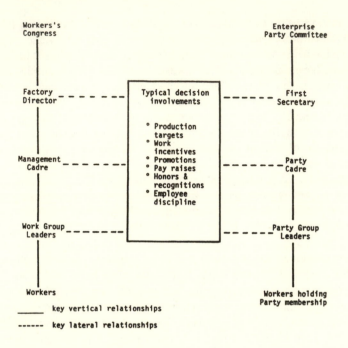

Figure 2. Parallel internal authority structures in the traditional
Chinese industrial enterprise

aging" and "disciplining" workers in job performance. *Controlling* was largely
an issue of ensuring conformity with the targets and budgets established by
state-mandated plans, and was accomplished with the direct involvement of the
party cadre on all matters of operating consequence.

Such historical legacies can make it difficult for true managerial leadership to
emerge within a firm. Subtle suggestions of this conclusion are found in Burton's
(1987) observation that the current reforms are designed to protect the status quo
of the Chinese Communist Party. The forces of stability, even in times of
change, therefore, run deep in this setting. They are found in an entrenched state
bureaucracy whose officials have tendencies toward retaining central control
(Henley and Nyaw, 1986b; Boisot and Child, 1988). They also exist in the
failures of some, perhaps most, factory directors to assume the authority commensurate with the responsibility made available to them under the reforms
(Petras, 1988; Boisot and Child, 1988).

This inherently conservative side of Chinese enterprises must be better understood—both to broaden the understandings of "outsiders" who seek to better
understand these enterprises and even conduct business with them, and to help
"insiders" establish an agenda for the development of enterprise managerial
leadership that is more realistic, given the prevailing conditions in China. Two

organizational phenomena of specific relevance here are the "substitutes for leadership" and "learned helplessness" effects.

Substitutes for leadership

Kerr and Jermier (1978) originally identified *substitutes for leadership* as the situation where organizational, individual, and/or task variables substitute for direct managerial leadership in work situations. They point out, for example, that formalization (of rules, roles, plans, and goals), inflexibility (rigidity in operating protocols and in applying rules and procedures), and well-developed staff functions (serving in advisory and directive roles) can all provide task direction for individual workers as a substitute for direct leader initiatives. In leadership theory, this concept is important because it offers a way for managers to avoid "redundant" leadership behaviors—that is, attempting to do something already provided for in the situation. Instead, it encourages them to provide "complementary" leadership behaviors that fill needs otherwise unmet by situational and individual variables. For the short run at least, past legacies may make this difficult to accomplish in Chinese enterprises.

Observation: The contemporary history of Chinese organizations includes many substitutes for leadership whose legacies continue to make it difficult to satisfy reform expectations for the development of more personal managerial leadership among members of the administrative cadre.

Because substitutes for leadership have operated in the past—based on the external state bureaucracy, the enterprise party structure, and the historical lack of managerial authority—many of China's present administrative cadre may have a "trained incapacity" for personal managerial leadership. Because such leadership substitutes continue to exist, it can and should be expected that Chinese institutions are by their very natures still "training" many of the cadre to be "incapable" of personal managerial leadership in the future. Chinese socialist traditions, for example, include an important place for "emulation campaigns" designed to increase workforce motivation. Whereas the administrative cadre are involved in these campaigns, "leadership" of them has largely rested with enterprise party officials serving the important party role of raising political consciousness and commitment among workers (Henley and Nyaw, 1987).

If and where the party proves willing to extricate itself from providing "substitutes" for managerial leadership, one has to inquire whether or not members of the administrative cadre have the expertise and/or willingness to fill the void. *If* and where the party is *un*willing to extricate itself from such leadership, one has to wonder what implications this holds for the ultimate assumption of complementary leadership roles by the administrative cadre. Past leadership substitutes in Chinese firms have the potential to constrain managerial development in the present and future, even under the most progressive of conditions.

Learned helplessness

"Alienation," "aimlessness," and "powerlessness" can develop among people who feel a lack of control over events shaping their lives. Social psychologists recognize that such feelings can arise in the workplace from a condition called *learned helplessness*. This is the tendency of persons who have been subject to tight controls, punishment for any misbehaviors, and repeated failures, to lose confidence that they have the skills required to succeed in their jobs (Martinko and Gardner, 1982, 1987). Learned helplessness occurs when a person learns from an experience of past inadequacies to feel incapable of future success.

Too many "signals" in the current Chinese economic and political environment foster learned helplessness and discourage personal leadership development among members of China's administrative cadre. In particular, the external state and party supervising external control over internal enterprise affairs has historically discouraged leadership initiatives by the administrative structure. Factory director Wu Changhai, for example, helped "turn around" the ailing Xian Food Machinery Factory (Clark, 1988). But he got into trouble with his superiors in the state bureaucracy after refusing their demands for what he considered an excessive share of his factory's new profits. They, in turn, harrassed him by sending in state inspection teams and encouraging workers to denounce him. Wu was taken off his job for more than a year. Instead of a "success" experience based on his managerial leadership initiatives, Wu experienced a "failure." For Wu and others like him, who now have the added experience of the 1989 Tiananmen events to consider, future reticence to display personal leadership initiatives is even more likely.

The organizational structures and policies, evaluation and reward systems, and goals typical to Chinese enterprises further establish learned helplessness conditions. In China, bureaucratic *structures and policies* in the past have led to tight external state controls and ever-present internal supervision by the party cadre. Organizational *evaluation and reward systems* in the past have not discriminated among workers on a true performance basis, and were often tied to issues of good "citizenship" behavior as interpreted by the party cadre. Enterprise *goals* in the past have been set by state plans and supervised through the external state bureaucracy and internal party cadre. Learned helplessness in these and other aspects of management can create frustration and passivity within the administrative cadre, even to the point where managers are unable to respond to new expectations and opportunities made available to them.

Observation: The contemporary history of Chinese organizations displays a tendency toward learned helplessness among members of the administrative cadre. This, in turn, makes it difficult for them to satisfy reform expectations for the expression of more personal managerial leadership.

Unfortunately, learned helplessness effects will most likely prove insidious and longlasting as they continue to "trickle down" throughout the management levels of any Chinese enterprise. Someone who is expected *not* to exercise initiative at one level of managerial responsibility is *not* likely to encourage it on the part of lower-level personnel, or to view it with much favor if so exercised by them. As a result of this self-reinforcing cycle of learned helplessness in the administrative ranks, Chinese firms can be expected to struggle for some time to come with performance limitations founded more on a lack of managerial leadership than on actual industrial potential.

Implications for research and leadership development

In order to better understand what is taking place within the Chinese industrial enterprises of today, one has to be aware of the historical and complex structural foundations from which Chinese firms are incrementally evolving. Substitutes for leadership and learned helplessness, both influenced by the role of the Chinese Communist Party in internal enterprise affairs, exemplify lingering constraints on the development of more truly personal managerial leadership by members of the administrative cadre.

Research implications

Management theorists should be cautious when framing their research questions and conceptualizations on Chinese organization and management practices. They should view the present aspects of Chinese industrial enterprises in the context of the past, and they should avoid premature conclusions based more on the allure of future possibilities than on current realities. A research agenda sensitive to such issues might address questions such as these.

1. What is the current role of the Chinese Communist Party as part of the parallel authority structure of enterprise decision making? In various industries and in organizations of various types, how is authority distributed between party and administrative cadre for managerial decisions? In what ways and under what conditions is the party role changing in respect to these decisions? In what ways is it remaining stable? What are the implications of the party's enterprise presence for organizational design and managerial leadership in the future?

2. Is there a difference between the managerial "leadership" required to achieve organizational effectiveness in each of the multiple and simultaneous systems of the Chinese industrial enterprise? If the typical Chinese factory director assumes a broader role than his or her Western counterparts, one that is more of the "mayoral" role described by Schermerhorn (1987), can the director provide effective leadership to both ancillary and business systems of the enterprise? Or, does the the Chinese firm operate with a group form of "executive office" responsible for ancillary as well as core business and commercial systems? If so, what are the consequences of this office and its political aspects to enterprise management and performance?

3. Which structures within Chinese industrial enterprises provide appropriate and inappropriate "substitutes for leadership"? What is known about past and present substitutes for leadership in Chinese organizations? What, if anything, can be done to maximize their advantages and minimize their disadvantages in the future? How is leadership responsibility in Chinese firms vested in people as opposed to structures, and to what extent is this investiture capable of changing in the present sociopolitical context of the economic reform environment?

4. What practices and conditions within Chinese industrial enterprises are still fostering the development of "learned helplessness" among the administrative cadre? How have the complex structures of the past and the traditional role of the party contributed to the emergence of learned helplessness? How pervasive is learned helplessness, and is there any "pattern" to its occurrence? What, if anything, can be done to overcome learned helplessness and establish true managerial leadership and confidence among China's administrative cadre?

Leadership development implications

To the extent that historical constraints on the development of managerial leadership are recognized in China, appropriate leadership development initiatives can and should be pursued. At the policy level, of course, the implications for change are complex and fundamental, especially in respect to the country's present political environment. Extreme limits on managerial leadership development seem indigenous to the prevailing system, especially now that the 1989 Tiananmen events have reconfirmed the strength of political influences over day-to-day affairs in all aspects of Chinese life. Yet at the level of enterprise operations, particularly in individual firms where special attention is given to improved management, modest initiatives of a leadership development nature may be possible.

Four training strategies identified by Martinko and Gardner (1982) for dealing more generally with learned helplessness may offer some potential short-run and local benefits. These strategies are:

1. Immunization training: Recognize that new entrants to the administrative cadre are likely to find that past legacies within the firm constrain leadership initiatives. Prepare them through training to expect these difficulties and to understand their personal reactions. Provide them with first-job managerial assignments that assure reasonable amounts of early success. This will help build their confidence for later dealings with more formidable leadership constraints at higher levels of managerial responsibility.

2. Discrimination training: Recognize that existing members of the administrative cadre will have special difficulty adapting to any changing expectations associated with management reforms. Increase their self-confidence by training them to better understand differences between past and present situations in the firm. Train and counsel them to understand how the future is expected to be even more different from the past and present, and to recognize the personal skills required to achieve managerial success in the future.

3. *Attributional training:* Recognize that the administrative cadre, already experiencing a sense of learned helplessness, is likely to view past leadership failures and difficulties as being caused by external forces beyond its control. Train them to better understand their individual strengths and weaknesses as managers, and to recognize personal avenues for change and development. Train them to better understand new opportunities, even very small ones, that exist within the firm, and which allow them to further develop their leadership abilities.

4. *Modeling training:* Recognize that members of the administrative cadre can benefit from "role models" who demonstrate the desired managerial leadership and offer day-to-day reinforcement for the leadership development efforts of others. Train "high-potential" managers to become more confident and capable leaders by assigning them to work with and for others in the firm who already display the desired leadership qualities. Make sure such role models are available at all levels of managerial responsibility in the firm.

Conclusion

Given the continuing novelty to the Western eye of reforms in the Chinese economic and political scenes, it has been tempting to interpret developments in enterprise management from a narrow perspective dominated by prospects for change. Yet there can be little doubt that the managerial leadership in state-owned Chinese industrial enterprises is limited by complex historical legacies of a structural and political nature. And while there certainly is some manifestation of personal managerial leadership among the administrative cadre in today's enterprises, it is unlikely that dramatic improvements in this important dimension of organizational life will occur either quickly or smoothly. China's past, simply put, holds too great a grasp on its present and future affairs—something demonstrated all too well in the 1989 Tianenmen massacre and party crack-down on the student-led "democracy movement." Management researchers and observers, accordingly, should give all due attention to the constraining legacies of traditional organizational practices and the role of the Communist Party on the emergence of managerial leadership in Chinese industrial enterprises.

Postscript

It is now July 1990. For all practical purposes, China's management and organizational reforms are still severely constrained in the aftermath of the June 4, 1989, Tiananmen disaster. The party is reasserting control over the country's institutions, and most enterprises seem to be taking "two steps back" on their difficult path to true industrial progress. Once again, it seems, enterprise managers must live with the "downside" of yet another of China's "speed-up and slow-down" cycles.

The difficulties of developing managerial leadership under such conditions are even more evident today than when our article was first drafted. After the turmoil and trauma of the past year, one has to wonder how members of the administrative cadre can sustain commitments to management and leadership development when their roles in enterprise affairs are subject to such externally-induced change and uncertainty.

By the time this postscript is read, some major transformation may have occurred to unlock the full productive potential of China's industries. It is more likely that social, political, and economic conditions will continue to limit both industrial development and the emergence of true managerial leadership in Chinese enterprises. As long as this continues to be the case, a great national resource—the managers of China's organizations—will remain largely under-utilized.

References

Bachman, D. (1988) "Politics and Political Reform in China." *Current History*, 87, pp. 249–256.

Boisot, M., and Child, J. (1988) "The Iron Law of Fiefs: Bureaucratic Failure and the Problem of Governance in the Chinese Economic Reforms." *Administrative Science Quarterly*, 33, pp. 507–527.

Burton, C. (1987) "China's Post-Mao Transition: The Role of the Party and Ideology in the 'New Period.' " *Pacific Affairs*, 60, pp. 431–446.

Byrd, W., and Tidrick, G. (1984) *Recent Chinese Economic Reforms: Studies of Two Industrial Enterprises*. Washington: The World Bank.

Clark, L. H., Jr. (1988) "China Must Avoid the 'Marble-boat' Syndrome." *The Wall Street Journal*, June 9, p. 28.

Cyert, R. M., and March, J. G. (1963) *A Behavioral Theory of the Firm*. Englewood Cliffs, NJ: Prentice Hall.

Frankenstein, J. (1986) "Trends in Chinese Business Practice: Changes in the Beijing Wind." *California Management Review*, 39, pp. 148–160.

Henley, J. S., and Nyaw, M. K. (1986a) "Introducing Market Forces into Managerial Decision-making in Chinese Industrial Enterprises." *Journal of Management Studies*, 23, pp. 635–656.

_____. (1986b) "Reforming Chinese Industrial Management." *Euro–Asia Business Review*, 5, pp. 10–15.

_____. (1987) "The Development of Work Incentives in Chinese Industrial Enterprises—Material versus Non-Material Incentives." Chapter 9 in M. Warner (ed.), *Management Reforms in China*. London: Frances Pinter Publishers.

Ignatius, A. (1989a) "Now if Ms. Wong Insults a Customer, She Gets an Award." *The Wall Street Journal*, January 24, p. 1.

_____. (1989b) "In this Factory Town, China's Welfare State Is Still Alive and Well." *The Wall Street Journal*, October 17, 1989, 1, p. 23.

Jiang, Y. (1980) "On the Leadership System of Socialist Enterprises." *Hongqi* [Red Flag], 21, pp. 9–13. (in Chinese)

Kasper, W. (1982) "Note on Sichuan Experiment." *The Australia Journal of Chinese Affairs*, 7, pp. 163–172.

Kerr. S., and Jermier, J. (1978) "Substitutes for Leadership: Their Meaning and Measurement." *Organizational Behavior and Human Performance*, 22, pp. 375–403.

Lai, G. T., and Lam, C. Y. (1985) "A Study on Work-Related Values of Managers in the People's Republic of China (Part II)." *Hong Kong Manager*, 22, 23–59.

Leung, J. (1989) "Socialism Burdens a Chinese Car Venture." *The Wall Street Journal*, April 13, A14.

Ma, H. (1980) "On the Reform of Industrial Enterprise Leadership System." *Jinqji Quanli* [Economic Management], 12, pp. 14–22. (in Chinese)

Martinko, M. J., and Gardner, W. L. (1982) "Learned Helplessness: An Alternative Explanation for Performance Deficits." *Academy of Management Review*, 7, pp. 195–204.

_____. (1987) "The Leader/Member Attribution Process." *Academy of Management Review*, 12, pp. 235–249.

Petras, J. (1988) "Contradictions of Market Socialism in China (Part I)." *Journal of Contemporary Asia*, 18, pp. 3–23.

Redding, S. G., and Wong, G. Y. Y. (1986) "The Psychology of Chinese Organizational Behavior." Chapter 7 in M. Bond (ed.), *The Psychology of the Chinese People*. Hong Kong: Oxford University Press.

Schermerhorn, J. R., Jr. (1987) "Organizational Features of Chinese Industrial Enterprise: Paradoxes of Stability in Times of Change." *Academy of Management Executive*, 1, pp. 345–349.

Shenkar, O., and Ronen, S. (1987) "Structure and Importance of Work Goals Among Managers in the People's Republic of China." *Academy of Management Journal*, 30, pp. 564–575.

Tung, R. (1982) *Chinese Industrial Society Post Mao*. New York: Lexington Books.

Warner, M. (1985) "Training China's Managers." *Journal of General Management*, 11, pp. 12–26.

_____. (1987) *Management Reforms in China*. London: Frances Pinter Publishers.

Zhu, Y. (ed.) (1985) *Contemporary China Economic Management*. Beijing: Shehui Kexue Chubanshe. (in Chinese)

Ruth L. Wang, Chiang Wang,
and Yingrong Gong

Enterprise Autonomy
and Market Structures in China

Introduction

For nearly thirty years, China's economic policies had been copied from the
Soviet model until the late 1970s. During this long period, the state took care of
all the revenues and expenditures of state enterprises and dictated all the material
purchase and output distribution. No enterprise was treated as an independent
accounting unit bearing responsibility for its own profits and losses. Since the
government believes that foodstuffs and basic industrial materials are essential to
the nation's economic stability and development, prices are fixed, and production and distribution are directly state-controlled for these product items. Depending upon how its outputs are classified, an enterprise is given a different
degree of management autonomy, based on which distinctive set of management
and marketing strategies will be devised. At one extreme, if an enterprise produces something that is 100 percent directive (directly controlled by the state),
there will be no need for the enterprise to be engaged in any marketing activities.
The economic reform was supposed to change the situation in which, for years,
some products were overstocked and many others were constantly in shortage.
But the step-by-step approach to enliven the once tightly controlled market has
been challenged by unanticipated market reactions in the last few years. In
October 1988, a rectification policy was established to call for cutbacks of non-
productive investments.

Unfortunately, these cutbacks only offer a temporary antidote against the
"overheated" economy. What complicates the market today is that there are
several market structures in existence as a result of various degrees of decision
autonomy in China's economy. The objectives of this study are threefold: (1) to
investigate the real nature of enterprise autonomy and market structures in
China; (2) to identify variables that dictate state planning, and (3) to examine

Ruth L. Wang and Chiang Wang are at the School of Business Administration, California
State University, Sacramento. Yingrong Gong is President of the Shanghai Publishing and
Printing College, Shanghai, PRC.

their possible effect on the classification of market structures to obtain some insights into the country's economic structure.

These variables were first used in Mun's study (1985) to analyze responses from fifty Chinese managers attending a training seminar in Hong Kong. Planners of a centrally controlled economy generally use the two criteria of (1) economic importance, such as people's basic needs, new technological development, energy projects, and defense industry, and (2) market adaptability, such as the number of target markets, complexity of marketing mix, demand–supply situation, percentage exported, level in the need of hierarchy, and degree of marketing research needed, as guidelines in determining product category, degree of enterprise autonomy granted, and the type of market structure suitable for the enterprise. Mun claims that the results of his study support such policy assumptions based on a descriptive percentage comparison of responses from the fifty managers surveyed. In this study, we attempt to further Mun's study by examining possible relationships between these guidelines and enterprise autonomy/market structures. A survey of managers from Shanghai's major state enterprises and neighboring township enterprises were conducted in the summer of 1986 to test the hypotheses that market structures and enterprise autonomy are dictated by the product evaluation based on its economic importance and market adaptability. Some managerial practices resulting from different levels of decision autonomy of these enterprises were also investigated. The following section discusses the existing market structures in China.

Market structures in China

China's market today can be classified into three or four categories, according to the type of state economic planning. The enterprise director's freedom to formulate his own marketing plan is also affected by this classification. Nowadays, there are three forms of economic enterprises permitted in China: private, collective, and state-owned. These enterprises are subject to various degrees of state regulations ranging from 0 to 100 percent. The state began allowing individuals and families to establish their own businesses in 1979. There is no limit to the profit a private enterprise can earn. Bureaucratic red tape is minimal. They are free to select, design, and advertise their products. Shortage of commodities (especially repair parts) is a common problem (Reeder, 1984). Interestingly, while some collective enterprises enjoy the freedom of private entrepreneurs, they are faced with less severe supply problems. Collective enterprises, unlike the popular Western belief that they are formed by a group of individuals who petition the state for permission to establish their business, are actually collective entities of several state enterprises to operate side-line businesses. In other words, they are not privately owned collectives and, therefore, have the advantages of material acquisition, technology-sharing, access of information available to state enterprises only, but a lesser degree of state intervention.

Table 1. Four socialist markets in China

	Type I *directly planned market*	Type II *indirectly planned market*	Type III *enterprise direct sales market*	Type IV *free market*
state planning	direct	indirect	indirect, with enterprise's own production and sales plans	none
buying and selling relationships	fixed	fixed/ variable	variable	variable
state production planning goals	mandatory	reference	none	none
pricing	fixed	fixed/ floating	floating/ negotiated	set by demand
sales	purchased and distributed according to the state plan.	a fixed predetermined quota purchased by the state	optional purchase by the state/ sell in the market.	sell in the free, open market.
ownership	state-owned/ collectives	state-owned/ collectives	state-owned/ collectives	collectives/ individual enterprises

Source: Mun Kin-Chok, *Marketing, Investment, and Management in China and Hong Kong*, p. 210.

Chinese economists also define enterprises based on the degree of state control: directives (controlled and directed by state), state guidance (indirect state control), and market adjustment (free of state regulation) (Ho, 1982; Lo, 1979; Xue, 1982). Accordingly, market structures in China can be classified into four different types of plan-based and market-based systems (Mun, 1985). Table 1 presents the four types of Chinese socialist market structures defined by Mun Kin-Chok.

Mun's classification explains why China's market structures are different from those existing in free-market economies, and why marketing in China could be difficult due to the enterprises' various degrees of autonomy in forming their own production and marketing strategies. The 400,000 state-owned enterprises operate in Type I, II, and III markets. All private enterprises and some collectives are allowed in the Type IV or free market. But private enterprises contributed only 24 percent of the total national sales in 1986 (Zhang et al., 1987). The number of collective enterprises is rising. Many new collectives are being established in rural township industrial areas and Special Economic Zones. The largest percentage of China's enterprises, however, is still state owned.

Theoretically, some state enterprises and collectives are able to operate in the Type III or direct-sales market, which allows for limited leeway in terms of setting sales goals, pricing, and promoting to the target markets. In reality, a direct-sales market may be more of a nominal policy than a thriving new form of market mechanism in many aspects.

For instance, officially less than one-fifth of the total output value in Shanghai is directly controlled by the state. But in certain industries, such as textile, machinery, and equipment, major outputs are almost 100 percent directives, including those exceeding the original state planning levels. In some cases, even products not within the state's directive plans are purchased by the state, instead of being sold in the open market. Cotton yarns, according to the regulation of the state department, should be under state guidance, or a Type II, indirectly planned item. But managers from some major textile mills in Shanghai complained that their extra cotton yarn production was all collected by the government. Officials at the Shanghai textile ministry explained that it was a result of production undercapacity and increased textile export. In order to ensure that factories relying on cotton yarns as major production input would meet planned output goals, mills making cotton yarns were deprived of their right to sell directly in the open market, since there was nothing left for them to sell. The same has occurred to many products classified into Type III or direct-sales market. In other words, both Type II and Type III markets—the partially plan-based, market-directed systems—are constantly under the risk of being forced back into Type I, the totally plan-based market structure, depending upon the situation in the current marketplace. The government's market regulation in such cases usually works against the enterprise's operating situation by ordering them to turn in all inventory when demand is rising, and leaving them alone when excessive supply occurs.

Hence market structures in China do not always reflect the interworkings of market forces. Reform advocates believe that enterprises should be less restricted by directives from the authorities and more receptive to market conditions. The aim is to induce enterprises to match production to demand. The following section discusses the study on enterprise autonomy, marketing activities, and market structures in China's largest industrial city, Shanghai, and its surrounding rural township enterprises. The effects of policy guidelines on market structures are also analyzed.

The study

In this study we surveyed eighty urban enterprises in Shanghai and interviewed ten township industries in Shazhou, a rising rural industrial center in southern

Jiangsu province in 1986. Of the eighty survey questionnaires received in Shanghai, sixty-six were usable. An identical test instrument was used in both Shanghai and Shazhou.

To assess an enterprise's activity in a particular market structure, percentages of state directives were used as numerical measurements of Type I, Type II, and Type IV market structures. Type III (direct-sales market) was not included, due to its currently debatable status. We thus redefine Type II as a market structure that entails indirect sales guidance.

In our survey, the planning criteria of economic importance and market adaptability are further described by the following attributes: people's basic needs, technological development, number of target markets, complexity of market mix, demand–supply situation, percentages exported, level in the need hierarchy (ranging from basic necessities to luxury items), and degree of marketing research needed. Each attribute was evaluated on a six-point scale ranging from important to unimportant, low to high, and so forth. An even-number instead of odd-number scale was used to eliminate the possible focus on the "middle choice." Since the Chinese encourage conformity, and a "middle position" or "unbiasedness" has always been the essence of traditional management philosophy (Ho, 1986), we opted for a scale without a midpoint to avoid potential bias. In order to obtain more information, the survey was followed by interviews and on-site visits.

I. Enterprise autonomy: urban enterprises vs. township collectives

Initial descriptive statistics reveal that none of the township enterprises interviewed were 100 percent directives, whereas 21 percent of Shanghai's urban enterprises fell into this category. Most Shanghai enterprises were of mixed forms of directives, state guidance, and partially adjusted by market forces. The majority of the township enterprises we interviewed in Shazou, however, operated completely according to the market situation. Only a handful (less than 10 percent) of Shanghai's urban enterprises had the autonomy of producing and selling to meet the market demand. Table 2 presents a contrast between urban and rural enterprises based on the three levels of management autonomy (directives, state guidance, and market adjustment).

When asked if they had any authority to appoint mid-level management personnel, most Shanghai and Shazhou enterprise leaders responded positively (83 percent and 90 percent, respectively, as shown in Table 3). However, the high percentage of urban enterprise managers' perception of their decision-making power may be overstated. Our data on sixty-six Shanghai urban enterprises were collected by distributing questionnaires to managers attending a seminar, where many respondents might have felt compelled to paint a brighter picture. More reliable information was revealed in the interviews we conducted later while touring the plants of half a dozen of the most prominent state enterprises in Shanghai. Factory managers of these enterprises complained about their lack of

Table 2. Enterprises classified by degrees of autonomy

degree of autonomy	type	urban enterprises (Shanghai)	township enterprises (Shazhou)
directives	completely	21%	0%
	mostly	39	10
	occasionally	6	30
	never	34	60
state guidance	completely	5	
	mostly	5	
	occasionally	45	
	never	45	
adjusted by market mechanism	completely	9	60
	mostly	8	30
	occasionally	36	10
	never	47	0

real decision-making power from raw material supply, production planning, and product distribution, to employment policy. Many admitted that the "enterprise managers' responsibility system" was a long way from being fully implemented. Most executive plant managers were still figureheads following orders from the party secretary of the plant, who in turn received directions from the party and state. In general, managers of these state enterprises either displayed some uncomfortable discontent or were reluctant to provide many personal opinions throughout the interviews.

On the contrary, the township enterprise managers we interviewed were more candid and quite optimistic about the future outlook of their organizations. They were also younger, though not necessarily better educated. The director of a Shazhou woolen mill proudly described his defiant act against the county government's order not to raise supervisors' salaries several hundred percent as a reward for their high productivity. His decision has not been punished by the county authority to date. In three years, the plant's total sales grew from 110,000 yuan to 8 million yuan.

Most township enterprise managers agreed they had real management power in hiring or firing workers, determining salary levels, and, most importantly, reinvesting profit for future expansion. Their greater authority is further evidenced by both urban and rural enterprise managers' assessment of middle-level management's decision-making power. More urban managers responded that their middle management can hire or lay off workers under their supervision (see Table 3). One possible explanation is that township enterprises are smaller and have no need to delegate decision power to lower levels since most enterprise directors can oversee the entire operation. This centralized decision-making process is, in fact, more efficient. Rural factories may be technologically inferior to

Table 3. Enterprise managers' responses to selected survey questions regarding enterprise operations and marketing activities

	urban enterprises (Shanghai)	rural enterprises (Shazhou)
Whether or not the enterprise director or factory manager personnel can appoint mid-level management	83%	90%
Whether or not middle management other than the enterprise director can hire or lay off workers under their supervision	54	43
Target Market:		
1. Shanghai and neighboring counties	16	10
2. Jiangsu and neighboring provinces	16	20
3. Nationwide	68	70
Does the enterprise engage in any exporting business?	50	30
Does the enterprise engage in any marketing research activities, including surveillance of market information?	56	90

state enterprises, but their rapid growth and greater adaptability are clear indications that efficiency cannot be attained unless enterprise leaders have the real power to run their organizations.

Table 3 also shows that about 70 percent of Shazhou's township industries sell their products to the vast nationwide market, and 30 percent export to international markets. The most striking revelation is that 90 percent of the Shazhou's rural enterprises are committed to marketing research activities, compared to only 56 percent of Shanghai's urban enterprises.

Most township enterprises are collectives. Moreover, they are not under the state's regulatory system. These township collectives are, in fact, operating in the Type IV or free market structure, in which many urban collectives do not belong. Visits to Shanghai's large state enterprises and Shazhou's township collectives were vastly contrasting experiences. In Shazhou, we noticed strong interests in marketing research and information gathering, although most efforts were focused on market surveillance and field observation, with little experience in survey techniques or in-depth study.

Township collectives were also quick in developing new products. Innovations were encouraged. Unlike the state enterprises' product-oriented production, they were increasingly more market oriented. State enterprises would produce undifferentiated products without improving product features for many years. Township enterprises, on the contrary, were often inquisitive about the latest design and development in the international market. They also communicated

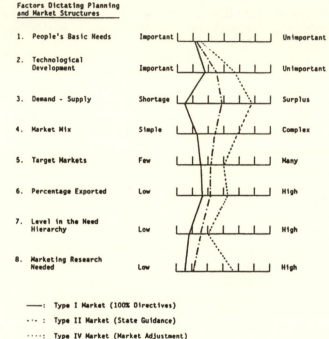

Figure 1. Administrative criteria and market structures

and negotiated with foreign businesses directly, whereas the foreign trade ministry handled exports and imports for state enterprises. Whether dealing with domestic buyers/sellers or foreign companies, township collectives negotiated and set their own prices; while state enterprises' prices were determined by the state planning committee or the foreign trade ministry.

Township enterprises we interviewed also indicated that they engaged in small-scale test marketing. They also provided before and after sales services. Quantity discounts were allowed to encourage large-volume sales, and personal selling was very popular. Many collectives had their own, aggressive sales forces. All the marketing activities described above were almost nonexistent in most state enterprises. A large share of the advertising we watched on Shanghai's TV broadcasting for over a month seemed to be commercials put together by collectives; many of them were township enterprises from southern Jiangsu and Jiejiang provinces.

II. Policy guidelines and enterprise autonomy/market structures

Although China's planning authority, enterprise directors and many researchers (Ho, 1982; Lo, 1979; Mun, 1985; Xue, 1987, 1982) believe that the degree of enterprise autonomy and market structures are determined by the two major criteria of economic importance and market adaptability, our study does not fully evidence such relationships. More precisely, the intent to establish an orderly planned commodity economic society (Xue, 1987) seems somewhat distorted in the actual practice.

Figure 1 presents profiles of the three different types of market structures based on the average responses of the seventy-six enterprises surveyed. For example, profile A depicts products that serve to meet people's basic needs, that are technologically important in the nation's economic development, in great demand, require the least complex marketing strategies, the least marketing research, and are least likely to be exported. These products receive 100 percent state directives, or are exchanged in the Type I market. The exchange process is in fact planned and not by choice. The Type IV market is just the opposite. Multiple regression analysis using percentage of directives as a measurement criterion and eight explanatory variables was also conducted. These attribute variables are (1) the product's importance in meeting people's basic needs, (2) the importance of technological development, (3) demand, (4) complexity of the product's marketing mix, (5) the number of target markets, (6) percentage exported, (7) level in the need hierarchy, and (8) marketing research needed for production planning. Although the profiles in Figure 1 are basically consistent with previous studies, the statistical analysis using multiple regression analysis reveals something else. The only factor that has a statistically significant effect on market structure is demand ($p < 0.05$). The greater the demand is, the more likely that a product will be placed in the Type I market. The other variables do not show a significant effect on market structure in the regression model, due to their high correlations with demand and among themselves. The factors such as complexity of marketing mix, number of target markets, percentage exported, and marketing research needed are rated as simple or low for the Type I market. This is more likely to be the result rather than the cause of state planning. Marketing under a strict state directive is made simple because there is no need for aggressive "marketing." Production and distribution are carried out according to a fixed, predetermined pattern. Attempts to use these factors (categorized by Mun as "market adaptability") to interpret the cause-and-effect relationship between product attributes and enterprise autonomy/market structure may be inappropriate.

In short, not only does the planning authority believe production and distribution of basic necessities and industrial materials should be directed by the state, but it also tends to put commodities in high demand directly under state regulation. Consequently, most state enterprises are not motivated to produce more, and no profits are retained—even when they are allowed nowadays—to reinvest for future expansion. Shortage becomes a perpetual problem if these highly demanded items are not allowed to be exchanged in a free market. This is probably one of the real underlying causes of China's recent inflation and excessive price increases.

Conclusion

The major findings of this study are twofold: (1) demand is the major factor dictating the degree of an enterprise's autonomy and its market structure—products in excessive demand are most likely to be regulated by the state; and (2) market structures of township collectives are less complex than those of urban enterprises (see Table 2). Rural township enterprises also enjoy greater flexibility in management decisions and are more active in the marketplace (see Table 3). This is not to say that township enterprises were not responsible for the runaway inflation in 1988. Quite the contrary, exchanges between state and township enterprises helped accelerate recent price increases.

Although Chinese officials claim much has been done since 1979 to relax the state's direct control, leaders of many state enterprises and some collective entities we interviewed were still frustrated by their lack of authority, ranging from production planning, employment, and management and raw material supply to the distribution and marketing of their outputs. Using demand as a major administrative criterion to regulate enterprise's economic activities creates a never-ending, vicious cycle of shortage and inflation, since those who have access to materials in great demand can always resell them at much higher prices. The existence of different types of market structures is a manifestation of man-made, imperfect competition. As a result, China's economy today is characterized by a dual structure, with a planned sector (such as raw materials allocated to the enterprises at lower, government-set prices), accompanied by a partially free exchange reflecting distorted demand and supply.

Since the conclusion of the Third Plenary Session of the 13th CPC Central Committee in 1988, a series of measures have been drawn up to cool off the "economic overheating." One of them is to restore price control on food products as well as raw and semi-finished materials that are in short supply (Dai, 1989). Although the Chinese government insists this does not mean that reform is being obstructed (Wu, 1988), progress on enterprise autonomy has been very limited in the past two years, due to many setbacks.

Besides, despite Chinese economists' recommendation to separate enterprise ownership from managerial power under the system of state ownership (Zhao, 1988), it seems that major state enterprises will remain in the Type I market, at least for the time being. The interaction of Type I, Type II, and Type IV markets, however, has resulted in "dual price systems," which is responsible for China's recent economic chaos.

An update of Chinese enterprises (*Ruth L. Wang*)

Moving into 1990, there seems to be a strong inclination of returning to central planning. The Type IV market, China's small but dynamic private sector, is shrinking. The number of workers in the Type IV market has fallen from 23 million at the beginning of 1989 to 19.4 million at the end of June. New taxes and regulations have been imposed on private businesses. Rural township enterprises have also dropped from 19 million to 16 million, and have been forced to lay off 14 million out of it 96 million employees under the current austerity. By and large, enterprises that enjoyed greater degrees of managerial autonomy are being penalized most severely under the recent political swing back to the left. On the other hand, the restoration of stricter central control in large state-owned enterprises would only make the Type I market bigger, but not economically better. The Chinese government admits that a fifth of all state-owned enterprises are operating at a loss. Although not all the central government's orders are fully carried out in the coastal provinces, economic activities have been stifled by the lack of progress in enterprise management.

References

Dai, Yannian. (1989) "Can Inflation Be Curbed?" *Beijing Review*, 35, February 13–26, pp. 7–8.

Ho, C.; Yang, Daonang; and Wu, Z. (1986) *Classical Chinese Management Theory*. Beijing: Hsin Hua Book Company.

Ho, Jiengzhang. (1982) "Planned Economy and Market Mechanism—Revisited." *Economic Research*, 6 (Beijing, China).

Lo, Kongmo. (1979) "On Planned Economy, Market and Other Issues." *The Relationship Between Planning and Market in a Socialist Economy*. Beijing: Chinese Social Science Publishing Company.

Mun, Kin-Chok. (1985) "An Integration of the Socialist Market and Planning in China." *Marketing, Investment, and Management in China and Hong Kong*, pp. 207–219. Hong Kong: Kwang Jing Publishing Company.

Reeder, J. A. (1984) "Entrepreneurship in the Peoples' Republic of China." *Columbia Journal of World Business*, 19, pp. 43–51.

Wu, Ge. (1988) "Policy of Reform and Openess Remains Unchanged." *Beijing Review*, 34, October 31–November 6, pp. 7–8.

Xue, Muqiao. (1982) *A Planned Economy Adjusted by Market Structure*. China: Ministry of Finance.

_____. (1987) "Socialism and Planned Commodity Economy." *Beijing Review*, 33, August 17–23, pp. 14–19.

Zhang, Hongji; Qiu, Xiaohua; and Yan, Kalin. (1987) "Reform Spurs Economic Development." *Beijing Review*, 33, October 19–26, pp. 21–22.

Zhao, Ai, and Wu, Ming. (1988) "Ten Theoretical Questions Facing Reform." *Beijing Review*, 34, August 22–28, pp. 24–27.

WILLIAM A. FISCHER, KATHRYN L. BLACKMON,
AND WILLIAM WOODWARD

Technical Decision Making in Chinese Enterprises

Along with personnel hiring decisions, the technical project selection decision is perhaps the most important determinant of ultimate innovative performance and climate within an organization. This should be no different in a planned or a market economy, in a developed nation or a developing one. The issue remains the same: the projects selected by the organization determine both the rate and the direction of the innovation that that organization supports. One might expect, however, that significant procedural differences would exist between innovative organizations in planned economies and those in market economies, and, also, between those in developing nations and those in developed ones. While the body of knowledge pertaining to R&D decision making (and to project selection methodologies in particular) pays little attention to this matter, the current economic reforms being experimented with in the PRC do provide an environment where some insights might be generated into both these questions. It also offers an opportunity to learn more about how the reform policies actually translate into operational decision making at the level of the Chinese industrial enterprise.

Chinese economic reforms and industrial decision making

One of the principal thrusts of the evolving economic reforms engineered by the Deng Xiaoping administration was the increased autonomy in decision making bestowed on China's enterprise managers (Fischer, 1986). Increasingly, the managers of Chinese enterprises had more decision realms opened up to them, and more alternatives within these decision realms from which to choose. The result has been startling and somewhat overwhelming. Whereas, not so long ago, a Chinese manager could be quoted as saying: "Working for the plan was so boring, you had no freedom, you didn't even have to think" (Kaspar, 1982), today there is widespread recognition of the new demands made on managers

William A. Fischer and Kathryn L. Blackmon are in the Graduate School of Business Administration, University of North Carolina, Chapel Hill. William Woodward is with Woodward and Associates, Chapel Hill, NC.

and frustrations over their inability to control all of the many dimensions of the managerial function (*China Daily*, 1986). As a result of the economic reforms, China has moved a long way from the period of the late 1960s (the Cultural Revolution period), when one Western observer (Bastid, 1973) was able to write: "Is there such a thing in China as an 'economic' decision?" to a point where influences on industrial decision making are both figuratively (Yang et al., 1987) and empirically (Chong, 1986) similar to those experienced in the West. Nonetheless, despite the apparent convergence that is taking place, China is still very much a system in transition, and as such provides the opportunity to draw comparisons among a variety of decision environments that are different from those typically seen in market economies.

China has long regarded itself as a centrally planned economy, and one of the hallmarks of central planning is the presumed ability of the state to organize and coordinate resource allocation and investment decisions in such a way that the key decisions are made outside the boundaries of the enterprise. This has been the case with respect to science and technology (S&T) in China, where there has been (at least since the early 1950s) an emphasis on central control and direction of all forms of R&D (Suttmeier, 1974). One of the results of this has been a pervasive reliance on "supply-push" dynamics (Suttmeier, 1982) to initiate and diffuse technological innovations.

Given the urgency of its needs and the absolute power that it commanded, it is not surprising that the Chinese government tended to favor such direct means of intervention as government funding of S&T, the reorganization of S&T resources into a command-type hierarchical system that focused on central research laboratories both in the Chinese Academy of Science, for basic research, and within each of the ministries, for directly relevant applied research, and the development of a variety of science and technology plans designed to coordinate and focus the efforts of China's S&T resources. Also reflecting supply-push inclinations were the establishment of mechanisms for the popularization of S&T and innovation. (Fischer, 1989, p. 121)

"Supply-push" strategies have characterized innovation in the Chinese electronics industry (Simon and Rehn, 1988; Pollack, 1985), the metallurgical industry (Yeh, 1985), and the textile industry (Tang, 1987). The result has been a significant loss in commercialization and utilization performance as the producers of R&D results have been isolated and estranged from the potential consumers of such innovations. The emphasis on increasing the influence of market forces, which is part of the centerpiece of the current reforms, is an explicit attempt to remedy this dysfunctional consequence of three decades of central planning.

One of the most prevalent symptoms of the pathologies of central planning for innovation has been the stereotype of being "risk averse." This stereotype has been widely applied to Chinese managers, and the characterization has been particularly frustrating for those interested in Asian economic development, because of the strong evidence of entrepreneurial values and behavior that exist elsewhere in this region (Redding, 1988). Despite historical cultural hospitality and encouragement for entrepreneurial action, it appears that the Chinese economic *system*, under socialism, has worked to discourage or suppress such behavior. The evidence appears everywhere: low productivity, poor quality and poorly designed products, slow decision making, and organizational cultures that discourage innovation (Fischer and Farr, 1985). As Dean (1979) has observed:

> It was not the cost of experimental development but rather the risk to production that deferred the chief engineer from introducing innovation. From management's point of view, any experimentation that involved production facilities was a risk to output and to fulfillment of production quotas in the state plan. Pressure to meet production quotas even caused management to avoid the trial-production assignments that were included in the state plan. (p. 10)

It would appear essential, if the reforms are truly to take hold, that the managers of Chinese enterprises regard the new operating environment as one that is not only different from the past, but, more importantly, one that is receptive to risk taking, more intimate relations with customers, and an aggressive, market-oriented behavior.

The study

Thinking about the issues mentioned above led the authors to revisit a database that was collected in 1983 and 1984, by the senior author, at the National Center for Industrial Science and Technology Management Development at Dalian in the PRC (Fischer, 1983). Despite the fact that this database is now more than six years old, there are certain characteristics about it that probably make it useful for understanding the Chinese situation at present. In particular, the database was collected from among managers of Chinese enterprises and ministries that were, at that point in time, at the forefront of the economic experimentation taking place. In many respects, being a pioneer in 1984 would create managerial situations that are representative of those being faced today by the average enterprise manager. Furthermore, China's economic reforms have been marked by hesitancy and reversals. As a result, the distance from 1984 to today is not as great as a linear chronological measure might suggest. Finally, this remains most likely the only sample of its type, and China remains a very difficult place to conduct survey research. Therefore, despite the age of the database, there does appear to be good reason to utilize it in developing insights into Chinese managerial behavior.

The sample of Chinese managers employed in this study consisted of eighty mid-level managers familiar with R&D project selection decisions in as many Chinese R&D units. The managers were representative of a wide range of industries and managerial situations. The managers were asked, as part of the survey,

Table 1. Twenty-eight criteria for project selection

PAST PERF	past performance of the enterprise in successful innovation
COMPAT	compatibility of the proposed project with existing business
NATL INT	importance to national interests
MGR TAL	managerial talent required for project success
MKT KNOWL	enterprise with market for proposed innovation
CAP INV	magnitude of capital investment required
RISK	magnitude of probable risk of failure
MKT SH	market share of enterprise in project business
SALES EST	estimated sales potential of the business
MKT REP	reputation of the enterprise in the market to be served
MFG CAP	manufacturing capabilities for project success
SUPPLIES	availability of necessary supplies
PROJ COSTS	costs associated with the project
SUCCESS	probability of project success
PROFIT	established profit potential of the project
MKT SKILLS	marketing skills and capabilities required for project success
TECH SKILLS	technical skills required for project success
DISTR SKILL	distribution skills for project success
COMPET	nature of competition within the market
PRICE STR	existing price structure within the market
PROD SCOPE	number of products/markets served by the project
TECH CHG	rate of technological change within the industry
POLI VISIB	political visibility of the project
TECH IMPR	improvement required in technical skills
PROTECT	ability to protect technology and advantages from competitors
WORK CAP	availability of working capital within the enterprise
PAYBACK	payback period associated with the project
INTL SOA	international state-of-art associated with the project

to appraise the relative importance of twenty-eight possible project (i.e., S&T projects considered by the enterprise's research institute or equivalent R&D organization) selection criteria (Table 1), for *each* of four different managerial situations.

    Case 1: radical projects that were generated outside of the enterprise;
    Case 2: incremental projects that were generated outside of the enterprise;
    Case 3: radical projects that have been generated internally by the enterprise;
    Case 4: incremental projects that have been generated internally.

The list of project criteria used in the study came from a longer list compiled by Bruce Merrifield (n.d.) as part of his development of a project selection methodology. For each criterion, in each situation, the respondents answered with a four-point Likert scale, ranging from 4 = "very important" to 1 = "not important."

Table 2. Criteria for project selection decisions

most important criteria	*least important criteria*
importance to national interests	nature of competition
technical skills required	existing price structure
improvements to the technical skills of the research staff as a result of working on this project	distribution skills
compatibility with existing business	number of markets served by product
magnitude of capital investment	

Overall results

When the sample is taken as a whole, the criteria in Table 2 appear as the most and least important for project selection decisions. Not surprisingly, for a society in transition from a strong reliance on central planning, the highest rated criteria reveal a lack of concern with profitability, a high concern for the availability of human resource skill, and the "fit" of a project with the prior experience of the organization. The lowest ranked criteria, on the other hand, reveal that competition is not important in a "seller's market," that the enterprise manager has little control over the prevailing price structure, and that there is little opportunity for market diversification.

The overall means, however, which led to the assignment of the criteria to the two columns in Table 2, mask serious disagreements within the survey sample for more than a few of the criteria. In particular, the standard deviations associated with such criteria as "sales potential," "political visibility," and "payback period" are high enough to suggest less than uniform consensus among the managers surveyed. This indicates that attention to the *context* in which the criteria are applied may very well be as important as the criteria themselves.

The context for project selection decisions

For radical projects that originate outside the enterprise, the three most important criteria were (1) the technical skills required, (2) the national interest involved, and (3) the market skills involved. These projects are those that are thrust upon the research unit rather than being selected by it; the unit has little choice about targeting markets or technologies. As is true of most radical innovations, the unit also has little past experience on which to draw, and often the technical skills that are required for the project are not available within the enterprise.

For incremental innovations that originate outside the enterprise, the mean scores on most criteria were much lower than scores for the other cases. These are technically less challenging projects, over which the enterprise has little control anyway. It is not a matter of deciding whether or not to take them; that decision has already been made and cannot be easily contested. The three most important criteria in these situations were (1) national interests, (2) market reputation, and (3) supplies. In this case, where the innovation is being imposed on the unit by an outside agency and where the change is not large, the ability of the enterprise to carry out the innovation without damaging its reputation appears to be the most important consideration.

For radical innovations that originate within the enterprise, mean scores were highest for (1) national interests, (2) capital investment, and (3) technical skills. As with the first case, technical skills and national interests are important. However, additionally in this case, as the impetus for the project is from within the enterprise, the magnitude of the required capital investment, and the wherewithal of the enterprise to finance the project, become important.

For those projects that are incremental and originate within the enterprise, (1) compatibility, (2) technical skills improvement required, and (3) project costs are most important. These are all factors that are important to consider if the innovation is to be supported successfully in commercialization.

In summary, several conclusions can be drawn:

1. Political considerations (national interests and political visibility) are more important than market considerations (market knowledge, market reputation, market skills, and market share) for projects imposed from outside the enterprise.

2. Financial considerations (sales estimates, project costs, profit, price structure, working capital, and payback) are more important for projects that originate within the enterprise than they are for projects imposed from the outside. This is not true, however, for capital investment considerations (which at the time of the survey were still largely provided to the enterprise as part of a grant economy).

3. Technical considerations (technical skills, technical change involved, degree of technical improvement, and international state of the art) are more important for radical innovations than for incremental innovations.

4. For innovations originating inside the enterprise, marketing considerations (marketing skills, market share, and market reputation) are more important for radical than for incremental innovations.

Concerns of the enterprises

The analysis above treated all of the project selection criteria as independent items. However, a more likely situation is for the manager to regard *groups* of project selection criteria as being related. Recognition of such behavior could change the importance and interpretation of the criteria examined in this study. Accordingly, principal components analysis was also used to see if interrelationships between project selection criteria could be identified that could provide better insights into the environment of technical decision making in Chinese enterprises. Principal components analysis results in the identification of linear combinations of the data that reduce the variance. Since the data were treated as exploratory in nature, the number of principal components to be identified was left free.[1]

Case 1: Outside radical innovations

For outside radical innovations, the five top principal factors identified were marketing acumen, financial considerations, market position, production ability, and political considerations. This indicates that for externally imposed radical innovations, the most important factors are the fit of the project within the market, and the enterprise's ability to support the project, rather than any concerns with its technical viability. Even though radical innovations may be assumed to require more technical skills than incremental innovations, these are rated fourth among the factors. It may very well be that the scientific issues involved with such projects are *spoken for* by the originator, leaving the performing enterprise only to worry about how they might capitalize on their participation.

Case 2: Outside incremental innovations

For outside radical innovations, the top five components are marketing position, market and technical visibility, infrastructure, cost recoupment, and cash flow. Incremental innovations generally involve less technical skill than radical innovations. Instead, the primary intent appears to be the ability to commercialize the innovation.

Case 3: Inside radical innovations

For inside radical innovations, the top five principal components identified were aggressiveness, riskiness, marketing acumen, financial attractiveness, and being a "sure bet." This pattern of factors may be interpreted as being the first on the market with a radical innovation, where the risk is not too high.

Case 4: Inside incremental innovations

For inside incremental innovations, market attractiveness, financial attractiveness, competitive edge, sourcing, and marketing capabilities are the five top principal components identified. These appear to be quite similar to what one would expect in a project selection review in a typical market economy environment.

Enterprise demographics

Along with *market context*, it seems likely that *enterprise* demographics will also be an important influence upon the way that different R&D projects are selected. By employing factor analysis to reduce the number of variables to be considered, an average score based on a variety of "enterprise demographic" characteristics was calculated. The demographic criteria considered were:

S&T focus: basic research, applied, development, or engineering
Industry stage: growth or mature
Number of R&D employees
Locus of control: centrally, provincially, or municipally led
Market importance: how important are market influences to the
  organization's R&D activities?
Total number of employees

For Case 1 (outside radical), increasing the number of R&D employees increased the importance of manufacturing capabilities, capital investment, and payback, while *decreasing* R&D size increased the importance of the ability to protect the market, magnitude of risk, payback, estimated sales, probability of success, and market share. Apparently, when dealing with radical projects that emerge from outside the enterprise, the larger R&D performers are more concerned about their ability to support the innovation *process*, while smaller R&D performers are concerned with their ability to support the innovation *product*. As the nature of the project becomes less basic and more applied, the importance of the ability to protect the technology, the magnitude of risk, and the potential profit involved all increase. This is not surprising, and is what might be expected in any type of economy. An increasing influence of market forces increased the importance of the ability to protect the technology, which is also understandable, given the desire to commercialize. An increasing influence of the market was also inversely related to the importance of market share, which may well reflect the "outside radical" nature of the innovation and the consequential reduced importance of the enterprise's *existing* market position. As the level of control over the enterprise moved upward in the economic system (i.e., toward the central government), manufacturing capabilities, international state of the art, and compatibility became less important, presumably reflecting the so-called "iron rice bowl" (*da guo fan*) that state organizations are criticized for taking advantage of. Increasing total numbers of employees were associated with a decreasing importance of the probability of project success, another indication of the luxury of size and state patronage in this economy.

In cases where radical innovations are originating from outside the enterprise, most market-oriented factors appear to decrease in importance, as does the importance of working capital availability. Again, this is not surprising, since such innovations are recognized as being risky and are probably well provided for by the sponsoring organizations. The desirability of such projects as means for upgrading the technical capabilities of the workforce does increase along with the more applied nature of such projects and the number of R&D employees.

Radical innovations originating within the enterprise tend to show a strong association with the availability of managerial talent, reflecting, no doubt, a recognition of the need to be able to produce and commercialize such R&D activities if they are to be worth the gamble. The more applied such projects are, the more such issues as market share and profit potential also come into importance. Interestingly, the importance of market influences to enterprises in such situations appears to *decrease* the value of the ability to protect such advances, market share considerations, market knowledge, and technical skill availability. Most likely, this occurs because of the *radical* nature of these projects.

In situations of incremental innovations that originate within the enterprise, competition, past performance, capital investment, risk, market knowledge, working capital, and payback period are the factors that are generated. Although they do not show much association with the demographic variables, the selection of these variables itself is instructive, as they indicate a focus, in such situations, on an ability to support the innovations on a day-to-day basis.

Conclusions

The survey results presented in this paper provide a number of insights into decision making in Chinese enterprises, which has been the subject of much speculative and anecdotal writing, but not, heretofore, subjected to empirical analysis. In particular, there are a number of decision criteria that ranked high in importance, which are clear legacies of central planning and which would not normally be seen in market-type economies. However, the importance of quite a few decision criteria changed substantially as the context of the decision changed (from, for example, internally generated to externally generated). In this regard, we should put to rest the old adage that "Chinese managers are risk averse." What the data clearly show are that Chinese managers address different decision situations in different ways. Finally, an analysis of enterprise demographic data also reveals a substantial legacy of central planning and affirms the existence of "iron rice bowl" thinking within the larger and more favored state enterprises. It is striking in this regard that internally generated projects lead to far fewer decision criteria experiencing *decreased* importance, relative to the enterprise demographic variables considered, than do externally generated projects.

All in all, the study reaffirms the rationality of Chinese management within the overall context of a centrally planned system. However, it also illustrates how different rationalities exist among economic systems. It suggests that major changes in decision making, reflective of the emergence of new decision contexts, were taking place when this survey was done. It also suggests that the transition occurring was not entirely free of contradictions and traditions that obscure the overall picture the outside observer gets. As we look back over the years that have passed since the survey was taken, one is struck by how prophetic the mixture of change and ambiguity portrayed by the survey has turned out to be.

Note

1. Principal components analysis was used with varimax rotation. The selection criteria for factor identification was the larger of the number of factors selected by the 75 percent variance rule or root curve analysis.

References

Bastid, M. (1973) "Levels of Economic Decision-Making." In S. M. Schram, ed., *Authority, Participation and Cultural Change in China*, pp. 159–197. Cambridge: Cambridge University Press.

Chong, L. E. (1986) "The PRC's Managers under the Self-Responsibility System. Developments in Managerial Decision Making in Chinese Industrial Enterprises." In S. R. Clegg, D. D. Dunphy, and S. G. Redding, eds., *The Enterprise and Management in East Asia*, pp. 305–312. Hong Kong: Centre of Asian Studies, University of Hong Kong.

Dean, G. (1979) *Technology Policy and Industrialization in the People's Republic of China*. Ottawa: International Development Research Center, pp. 23–24. As quoted in D. F. Simon and D. Rehn (1988), p. 10.

Factory Directors "Fed Up." (1986) *China Daily*, August 26, p. 3.

Fischer, W. A. (1983) "The Management Center at Dalian." *China Exchange News*, June 11, pp. 12–14.

_____. (1986) Chinese Industrial Management: Outlook for the Eighties. in Joint Economic Committee of the U.S. Congress, *China's Economy Looks toward the Year 2000*. Washington, D.C.: U.S.G.P.O., pp. 548–570.

_____. (1989) "China's Industrial Innovation: The Influence of Market Forces." In D. F. Simon and M. Goldman, eds., *China's New Technological Revolution*.. Cambridge, MA: Harvard University Press, pp. 119–135.

Fischer, W. A., and Farr, C. M. (1985) "Dimensions of Innovative Climate in Chinese R&D Units." *R&D Management*, July, pp. 183–190.

Kasper, W. (1982) "Note on Sichuan Experiment." *The Australian Journal of Chinese Affairs*, 7, pp. 163–172. As quoted in J. S. Henley and Mee-Kau Nyaw (1986), "Developments in Managerial Decision Making in Chinese Industrial Enterprises." In S. R. Clegg, D. C. Dunphy, and S. G. Redding, eds., *The Enterprise and Management in East Asia*. Hong Kong: Centre of Asian Studies, Hong Kong, p. 274.

Merrifield, B. (n.d.) Project Selection Criteria. Unpublished paper.

Pollack, J. D. (1985) *The Chinese Electronics Industry in Transition*. RAND Note N-2306. Santa Monica, CA: RAND Corporation.

Redding, S. G. (1988) "The Role of the Entrepreneur in the New Asian Capitalism." In P. L. Berger and H. M. Hsiao, eds., *In Search of an East Asian Development Model*. New Brunswick, NJ: Transaction Books.

Simon, D. F., and Rehn, D. (1988) *Technological Innovation in China*. Cambridge, MA: Ballinger.

Suttmeier, R. P. (1974) *Research and Revolution*. Lexington, MA: D. C. Heath.

_____. (1982) Science and Technology in China's Socialist Economic Development. Paper prepared for the World Bank Science and Technology Advisory Unit, Project Advisory Staff. January.

Tang, Z. (1987) "Supply and Marketing." In G. Tidrick and J. Chen, *China's Industrial Reform*, pp. 210–236. A World Bank Research Publication. New York: Oxford University Press.

Yang, G.; Lin, B.; Wang, H.; and Wu, Q. (1987) "Enterprise Cadres and Reform." In B. L. Reynolds, ed., *Reform in China*, pp. 82–83. Armonk, NY: M. E. Sharpe.
Yeh, K. C. (1985) *Industrial Innovation in China with Special Reference to the Metallurgical Industry*. RAND Note N-2307. Santa Monica, CA: RAND Corporation.

LEE A. GRAF, MASOUD HEMMASI, JOHN A. LUST,
AND YUHUA LIANG

Perceptions of Desirable Organizational Reforms in Chinese State Enterprises

A Managerial Perspective of the Challenges Ahead

Cultural values and belief systems produce significant differences in work expectations and job attitudes. The work values, managerial expectations, and job satisfaction of American managers have been compared with those of managers in a number of other countries (e.g., Alutto and Coleman, 1987; Chang, 1985; England and Negandhi, 1979; Hofstede, 1984; Slocum and Topichak, 1972). However, despite this growing body of comparative management research, lack of access to the world's most populated country, the People's Republic of China (PRC), has limited the ability of researchers to examine Western paradigms of work values and attitudes in a context that presents a sharp contrast to Western democracies.

The reopening of the People's Republic to the West in the late 1970s has led to increasing access to information and to an increased ability to conduct research. Despite the recent interest, however, access to sites for empirical research is still very limited. As a result, with the exception of a few studies (Alutto and Coleman, 1987; Graf et al., 1988; Laaksonen, 1984; Pegels, 1987; Seybolt et al., 1986; Shenkar and Ronen, 1987), the scant literature on China remains largely anecdotal in nature (see, for example, Daniels et al., 1985; Helburn and Shearer, 1984; Nelson and Reeder, 1985; Nevis, 1983; Tung, 1981; Warner, 1986).

Chinese work values and organizational philosophies, as well as managerial practices, are currently undergoing rapid change. Beginning with the "policy of economic readjustment" approved in December of 1978, the pursuit of the "Four Modernizations" has caused changes in the processes employed by Chinese work enterprises. Increased use of rewards and incentives (Nelson and Reeder, 1985;

Lee A. Graf, Masoud Hemmasi, and John A. Lust are in the Department of Management and Quantitative Methods at Illinois State University, Normal, IL. Yuhua Liang is at the Changchun Institute of Optics and Fine Mechanics, PRC.

Helburn and Shearer, 1984), changes in worker participation in management of the organization (Helburn and Shearer, 1984; Laaksonen, 1984), an increased focus on performance and productivity (Nelson and Reeder, 1985), and a de-emphasis of job security (Associated Press, 1988) have challenged the traditions employed since 1949 in Chinese work enterprises.

Despite these recent developments, China is a country with a long history and deeply rooted cultural values. Traditional Chinese philosophies, such as Confucianism, still guide individual actions and attitudes (Tung, 1981; Adler et al., 1986; Shenkar and Ronen, 1987). With the increasing contacts with the West, a clearer understanding of the contrast between current reforms and historic attitudes and philosophies is needed.

The purpose of this research is to evaluate managerial perceptions of the changes occurring in Chinese work enterprises. The present study assesses the existing organizational and managerial conditions in these enterprises. It then analyses managerial perceptions of how these organizational conditions "ought to be" ideally, and subsequently identifies the areas in need of change.

Managers in China's research institutes were chosen as the sampling unit for this study. These institutes are unique and crucial for China's economic development, because they are responsible for the bulk of the research and development activities which occur. Typically, these research enterprises have affiliated production facilities where prototypes are developed, tested, and prepared for final mass production. The significance of research enterprises is reflected by the fact that they now share in profits of factories that benefit from institute discoveries (Klass, 1983). In addition, there is growing recognition on the part of Chinese central policy makers that the current form of management of scientific and research personnel does not work well (Klass, 1983; Warner, 1986). Finally, the institutes are in the forefront of management development in the country. Thus, the perception of research managers provides not only an indication of reforms currently under way in PRC, but, perhaps more importantly, signifies the direction of changes to come.

Methods

Sample

The sample for this study is 239 managers from 9 of the 100 research institutes affiliated with the Chinese Academy of Sciences. The research institutes in this sample are geographically dispersed and are located in Anhui, Changchun, Chengdu, and Xi'an.

The sample is predominantly male (174 of the 239), ranges in age from 21 to 60 (mean = 41.5 years), and has an average of 14 years of formal education. The sample is dispersed across three management levels (66 supervisors, 137 middle, and 35 top level managers).

Procedure

The data were collected through a questionnaire as part of a larger project carried out in the fall of 1987. All responses were anonymous. Of the 512 questionnaires distributed, 239 were returned for a response rate of roughly 46 percent. The questionnaire was developed in English and translated into Chinese. To safeguard against the risk of non-equivalence in translation (Brislin, 1970), the questionnaire was translated into Chinese and back-translated to English by two independent bilingual translators.

Measures

In order to measure the managers' perceptions of the current work setting, data regarding several facets of the organizational work environment were collected. Specifically, information was obtained on degree of formalization and structure, reward and motivational processes, degree of cooperation exhibited, communication processes, interpersonal relationships, and security and stability in the organization. In all, 21 items were used. The respective items were adapted from Kelley et al. (1986), after discussion with several Chinese scholars to ensure that the concepts were understandable and relevant to worklife in the People's Republic. The items are shown in Table 1. The individual items were arranged randomly throughout the questionnaire.

The subjects responded to each item, based on their perceptions of how things "actually are" as a baseline, and then how conditions "should be." Both responses were made on seven-point scales, with 1 indicating minimum and 7 maximum presence of each condition. The differences between the "actual" and the "ideal" point toward the nature and direction of change.

Data analysis

Paired *t*-tests were used to assess mean differences between existing and preferred states. In addition, ANOVA was used to ascertain if results varied based on demographic characteristics (age, gender, etc.).

Results

Table 1 contains the mean responses for each item. Sample size varies for some items because of missing data, and ranges from 232 to 239. The first column shows the results for the existing setting, while the second column contains the mean responses for the preferred situation. The third and last columns represent mean differences as well as the resulting *t*-values. With the exception of items 8, 11, and 18 (i.e., manager consults subordinates, subordinates question authority, and company provides job security), all differences are statistically significant ($p > 0.001$).

Table 1.   Questions, means, standard deviations, differences, and paired _t_-test values

items	is now mean (s.d.)	should be mean (s.d.)	Diff.	t
Structure/formalization:				
1. Work objectives are made explicit.	4.19 (1.58)	5.89 (1.09)	1.70	14.80
2. Establishing and meeting work deadlines is expected of me.	4.86 (1.52)	6.06 (1.07)	1.20	11.34
3. Managers in this organization spend time preparing formal plans such as budgets.	3.85 (1.61)	6.18 (0.85)	2.33	20.82
4. In this organization, policies and procedures are followed.	4.26 (1.45)	6.19 (0.90)	1.94	19.13
5. In this organization, job duties are described by written procedures.	4.21 (1.46)	6.20 (0.91)	1.99	19.71
Atmosphere/relationships:				
6. Managers in this organization take an interest in personal problems of their subordinates.	3.68 (1.56)	6.00 (1.08)	2.32	20.27
7. Employees in this organization are afraid to disagree with their boss.	4.54 (1.62)	3.78 (1.95)	−0.76	−4.72
8. Managers in this organization make most decisions without consulting subordinates.	3.99 (1.52)	3.72 (1.95)	−0.27	−1.71 (ns)
9. Managers in this organization socialize with their subordinates after work.	3.29 (1.31)	5.29 (1.23)	2.00	18.81
10. In this organization, respect is given to one's position in the organization.	4.96 (1.61)	3.62 (2.00)	−1.34	−8.39
11. In this organization, there is little questioning by subordinates of the authority of their superiors.	4.15 (1.47)	4.29 (1.74)	0.14	0.77 (ns)
Rewards/motivation:				
12. In this organization, employees are rewarded based on their accomplishments rather than their seniority	3.45 (1.60)	5.88 (1.47)	2.43	15.86
13. Employees in this organization are motivated to improve their work performance.	4.28 (1.40)	6.26 (0.84)	1.98	21.28
Cooperation:				
14. Individuals in work groups in this organization tend to work together more than to strive for individual recognition.	4.10 (1.63)	5.91 (1.22)	1.81	14.43
15. This organization rewards cooperative behavior.	4.56 (1.45)	6.12 (1.03)	1.56	16.17

Table 1. (continued)

items	is now mean (s.d.)	should be mean (s.d.)	Diff.	t
Communication:				
16. Work objectives in this organization are clearly communicated to employees.	4.23 (1.42)	6.32 (0.79)	2.09	21.80
17. In this organization, employees are frequently given feedback about their work performance.	3.33 (1.30)	6.08 (0.89)	2.75	28.69
Security/stability:				
18. This company provides job security for its employees.	5.33 (1.36)	5.36 (1.69)	0.03	0.27 (ns)
19. In this organization, managers and workers like to see change in their jobs.	5.33 (1.20)	6.36 (0.70)	1.03	13.46
20. Managers in this organization take initiative and do things on their own.	4.58 (1.44)	6.26 (0.84)	1.68	17.47
21. Employees work in this organization a long time.	5.96 (1.20)	4.38 (1.88)	-1.58	-12.03

Note: All differences are statistically significant at the $p < 0.001$ level, except the three which are marked as not significant (ns).

Formalization/structure

The existing literature on management in China, predominantly developed through personal interviews and observations, paints a picture of Chinese enterprises as highly formalized and bureaucratic. As such, explicit work instructions are given to employees (Nelson and Reeder, 1985; Tung, 1981), and expectations regarding end results are usually made clear (Tung, 1981). In addition, Chinese organizations are characterized by a tight set of business rules and close supervision of the workforce (Adler et al., 1986; Nelson and Reeder, 1985).

The managers in this study tend to hold similar perceptions. For the existing situation, most of the means are close to 4 (on a 7-point scale) indicating a moderate presence for all of the factors (items 1, 3, 4, and 5: explicit objectives, formal planning, following policies, written procedures). The exception is item 2, establishing and meeting work deadlines. The mean for this question is almost 5, indicating that the managers surveyed perceive a significant use of and adherence to timetables and deadlines. It is interesting that these managers desire a greater degree of structure in the workplace. All means for the "should be" items are near 6, and the differences are all significant at $p > 0.001$.

Atmosphere/relationships

This area of the Chinese system presents an intriguing picture. Worker participation in decision making has historically been encouraged in the PRC (Laaksonen, 1984; Helburn and Shearer, 1984; Nelson and Reeder, 1985). The nature of this participation, however, has changed since 1978. During the Cultural Revolution, employees were involved, at least nominally, in enterprise decisions through "revolutionary committees" (Laaksonen, 1984). These committees were set up at different levels in the enterprise, and their structure paralleled that of the Communist Party's committees. However, the enterprise committees had little real power since the important decisions (production levels, prices, etc.) were made by central party officials (Laaksonen, 1984). Since 1978, participation has been encouraged through the more democratic workers' congresses. Members of these groups are elected by enterprise workers and managers (Helburn and Shearer, 1984), and have more real power than the revolutionary committees because of the greater independence of enterprises in decision making (Laaksonen, 1984). While the Chinese management system continues to evolve, Nelson and Reeder (1985) report that it is still somewhat autocratic and hierarchical, making it difficult to incorporate significant levels of individual participation. In addition, there appears to be employee reluctance to confront superiors individually (Nelson and Reeder, 1985), although employees may do so through the workers' congresses.

The managers in this study agree with the above-mentioned observations of Nelson and Reeder. There does not seem to be a high degree of consultation with subordinates in managerial decision making, and there remains worker reluctance to question authority (both items 8 and 11 have means near 4). In addition, the current level of subordinate consultation (difference = -0.27, ns) and the authority relationship between superiors and subordinates (difference = 0.14, ns) are viewed as satisfactory. Also, there is great respect given to authority positions (mean near 5 for item 10); and, as Nelson and Reeder (1985) suggest, employees are reluctant to disagree with their supervisors (mean = 4.54 for item 7). In both these areas, the managers call for improvement. These managers perceive a need to reduce the status attached to formal positions in the organization (difference = $-1.34, p < 0.001$) and to diminish fear of disagreement in the workplace (difference = $-0.76, p < 0.001$). This result points to a desire to increase worker independence and lower some of the existing barriers that may restrict that independence. The evolving political climate will dictate whether this change can occur.

Finally, as might be expected from the formality of the work situation, interpersonal relationships are somewhat limited. There seems to be a perception that managers and subordinates are isolated socially (item 9, mean = 3.29) and that managers are not concerned with the non-work-related problems of employees (item 6, mean = 3.68). These managers perceive that both areas should be improved. They suggest taking greater interest in the workers' personal problems (difference = 2.32, p < 0.001), and increasing informal socialization (difference = 2.00, p < 0.001). Thus, the managers recognize the impersonality of the current situation and favor increased attention to the workers.

Rewards/motivation

Organizational reward and motivation practices are another area undergoing change. For example, the increased use of bonuses to supplement the existing wage structure has radically altered pay practices (Tung, 1981; Klass, 1983; Helburn and Shearer, 1984; Nelson and Reeder, 1985). Despite the increasing use of incentives in Chinese enterprises, these managers still perceive that rewards are based not on accomplishments but on seniority (mean = 3.45). They perceive a moderate level of motivation in the workforce (mean = 4.28), and that both rewarding accomplishment and the general level of motivation should increase ("should be" means = 5.88 and 6.26, respectively).

Chinese wage policy is guided by two principles (Tung, 1981). On the one hand, there is opposition to a wide wage spread, as reflected in a differential of only 12 times between the lowest paid worker and the highest paid officials. On the other hand, there is adherence to the socialist principle of "from each according to his ability, to each according to his work." Our sample managers appear to be in agreement with the latter principle.

Cooperation

Cooperation is promoted, although competition between groups and organizations is also encouraged (Adler et al., 1986; Tung, 1981). The managers in this study do perceive that a moderate level of cooperation exists (mean = 4.10) and that collaborative behavior is reinforced (mean = 4.56). Again, though, this area shows need for improvement. These managers desire even more cooperation ("should be" = 5.91, difference = 1.81) and feel that teamwork should be increasingly rewarded ("should be" = 6.12, difference = 1.56).

Communication

The communication system in work enterprises is established to encourage interaction between managers and workers at all levels. Frequently, however, this open communication does not occur in practice and restrictions are sometimes developed (Nelson and Reeder, 1985). The sample managers perceive that a moderate level of communication of work objectives does exist (mean = 4.23), but that feedback on performance is clearly inadequate (mean = 3.33). As expected, these managers suggest a need to improve significantly in both areas. The differences for both items (2.09 and 2.75, respectively) are among the largest found in this study.

Security/stability

Finally, stability and security in the workplace present some of the most interesting results in this study. Consistent with the "iron rice bowl" philosophy, these managers perceive a high degree of employee stability in the workplace (item 18, company provides job security, mean = 5.33; item 21, employees work in this company a long time, mean = 5.96). Currently, a worker can only be discharged for a serious offense such as criminal conviction (Helburn and Shearer, 1984). However, the subject managers see a need for a change in this system. While they do not oppose job security (difference = 0.03, n.s.), they see much less need for a worker to remain in the same job/organization over the long run (difference = −1.58). This latter concern may stem from a desire for greater worker mobility. A worker's ability to change a place of employment is now limited by governmental assignment to jobs, lack of housing, etc. (Helburn and Shearer, 1984). Also, the data suggest that managers display considerable initiative (mean = 4.58) and that change on the job is welcomed (mean = 5.33). However, for both of these items, the managers see a need for further improvement (differences = 1.68 and 1.03, respectively).

Subgroup analysis

As mentioned earlier, ANOVA was also performed to determine if subgroup differences exist. No differences were found based on age and gender, and there were only minor differences based on education and organizational level. More educated individuals differed from the group as a whole in that they felt that managers should display a more participative style (managers do not consult, "is now" = 3.95; "should be" = 3.31, difference = − 0.64, $p < 0.009$). This result indicates a desire for increased involvement of employees in decision making. In addition, unlike the group as a whole, top managers felt a need for increased job security ("is now" = 5.23, "should be" = 6.00, $p < 0.001$). No other group differences were found.

Conclusions

Research institutes play a key role in China's economic development and appear to reflect the state of the art in that country's organizational and management practices. As such, the perceptions of managers of these institutes provide not only an indication of current conditions, but also point to directions for future reform. The managers, for example, express a need for greater reliance on formal plans and the application of uniform policies and procedures to guide managerial actions. They also call for a more participative style of management combined with greater tolerance for disagreement, independence, and dissent. Communications, superior–subordinate relationships, and organizational reward systems appear to require the greatest change (judged by the magnitude of the discrepancies between "actual" and "ideal" conditions). These managers suggest that not only should work goals be made explicit and communicated to workers, but also that more frequent feedback on actual performance be provided to employees. Moreover, rewards have to be commensurate with the individuals' accomplishments and their contributions to the achievement of organizational objectives. And, finally, managers not only should be encouraged to interact with employees, but also to take greater interest in them and their problems at a more personal level.

In short, the study participants suggest that the managing of Chinese enterprises must, in the future, adhere more to what Western organizational literature recognizes as "principles of effective management." With the increasing allocation of resources to management training and development in recent years (Warner, 1986), it appears that steps are being taken to equip organizations to deal with the aforementioned problems. One may question if the recent policy shift in the PRC will alter the results of this study. The changes seem to be a clarification of political policy and not a reversal of economic reforms (Silk, 1989; Schmetzer, 1989). Thus, while it is speculation, the authors do not expect a change in the economic reforms occurring in China.

Acknowledgment

This research was partially supported by a grant from Illinois State University. In addition, the authors wish to thank Professor Wang Qingyun, Miss Liang Airong, Miss Xu Qin, and Mr. Yin Yingqi of the Changchun Institute of Optics and Fine Mechanics for their help with the data collection process.

References

Adler, N. J.; Doktor, R.; and Redding, S. G. (1986) "From the Atlantic to the Pacific Century: Cross-Cultural Management Reviewed." *Journal of Management*, 12, pp. 295–318.

Alutto, J. A., and Coleman, D. F. (1987) "Cross-Cultural Examination of Perceived Job Characteristics of Chinese Managers." In C. Pegels (ed.), *Management and Industry in China*. New York: Praeger Press.

Associated Press. (1988) "China Prepares for Unemployment." *Chicago Tribune*, October 16, Section 1, p. 10.

Brislin, R. W. (1970) "Back Translations for Cross-Cultural Research." *Journal of Cross-Cultural Psychology*, 1, pp. 185–216.

Chang, S. C. (1985) "American and Chinese Managers in U.S. Companies in Taiwan: A Comparison." *California Management Review*, 27, pp. 144–156.

Daniels, J. D.; Krug, J.; and Nigh, D. (1985) "U.S. Joint Ventures in China: Motivation and Management of Political Risk." *California Management Review*, 27, pp. 46–58.

England, G. W., and Negandhi, A. R. (1979) "National Contexts and Technology as Determinants of Employees' Perceptions." In England, Negandhi, and Wilpert (eds.), *Organizational Functioning in a Cross-Cultural Perspective*. Kent, OH: Kent State University Press.

Graf, L. A.; Hemmasi, M.; Liang, Y.; and Tcheng, M. (1988) *Work Values, Work Importance, and Job Attitudes of Chinese Managers: An Exploratory Investigation.* Paper presented at the national meeting of the Decision Sciences Institute, Las Vegas, NV.

Helburn, I. B., and Shearer, J. C. (1984) "Human Resources and Industrial Relations in China: A Time of Ferment." *Industrial and Labor Relations Review,* 38, pp. 3–15.

Hofstede, G. (1984) *Culture's Consequences* (abridged ed.). Beverly Hills, CA: Sage Publications.

Kelley, L.; Whatley, A.; Worthley, R.; and Lie, H. (1986) "The Role of the Ideal Organization in Comparative Management: A Cross-Cultural Perspective of Japan and Korea." *Asia Pacific Journal of Management,* 3, pp. 59–75.

Klass, P. J. (1983) "Chinese Push Managerial Improvement." *Aviation Week and Space Technology,* June 20, pp. 68–72.

Laaksonen, O. (1984) "Participation Down and Up the Line: Comparative Industrial Democracy Trends in China and Europe." *International Social Science Journal,* 36, pp. 299–318.

Nelson, J. A., and Reeder, J. A. (1985) "Labor Relations in China." *California Management Review,* 27 (4), pp. 13–32.

Nevis, E. C. (1983) "Cultural Assumptions and Productivity: The United States and China." *Sloan Management Review,* 24 (3), pp. 17–28.

Pegels, C. C. (1987) *Management and Industry in China.* New York: Praeger Press.

Schmetzer, U. (1989) "Brush with Economic Reform Goes Begging." *Chicago Tribune,* November 5, Section 7, p. 1.

Seybolt, J. W.; Zhou, N.; and Wu, Y. (1986) "A Preliminary Investigation of the Work Attitudes and Motivation of Managers in the People's Republic of China." In *Proceedings of the 1986 Annual Meeting of the Decision Sciences Institute,* pp. 102–104.

Shenkar, O., and Ronen, S. (1987) "Structure and Importance of Work Goals among Managers in the People's Republic of China." *Academy of Management Journal,* 30, pp. 564–576.

Silk, L. (1989) "Turbulent Days for Communism." *New York Times,* June 30, Section D, p. 2.

Slocum, J. W., and Topichak, P. M. (1972) "Do Cultural Differences Affect Job Satisfaction?" *Journal of Applied Psychology,* 56, pp. 177–178.

Tung, R. L. (1981) "Patterns of Motivation in Chinese Industrial Enterprises." *Academy of Management Review,* 6, pp. 481–489.

Warner, M. (1986) "Managing Human Resources in China: An Empirical Study." *Organization Studies,* 7, pp. 353–366.

Sally Stewart and Chong Chung Him

Chinese Winners:
Views of Senior PRC Managers
on the Reasons for Their Success

Nothing yet appears to have been published on the "self concept" (to use Norburn's 1987 phrase) of Chinese managers. This study was, therefore, designed to examine what characteristics Chinese top managers themselves believed were most important for a successful career, and to try to contrast their views with findings relating to Western managers. Why managers themselves think they have made it to the top of their organizations casts a light on their values and attitudes which may be of use to those doing business in the People's Republic of China (PRC). It may also indicate what qualities they look for when promoting junior managers and this, in turn, may help those concerned with management training in China.

The necessity for understanding the attitudes and values, the "culture" within which management development is undertaken, is, as Kirkbride, Tang, and Shae (1989, p. 8) put it, a "fairly obvious assertion." They stress that "it is obvious that culture does create barriers or set limits to the transferability of managerial concepts, practices, procedures, and to management training and development in general." It is hoped that this paper may indicate some of the limits on transferring Western concepts and methods to Chinese managers, and, also, perhaps, show in what areas some of the managers could benefit from training.

Not all successful Chinese managers (any more than Western ones) feel they necessarily need development. This was vividly demonstrated in a volume of "faithful oral accounts . . . based on taped or recorded interviews" (Zhang and Sang, 1986, Foreword), which had a profile of a manager who in four years "turned a street committee-run repair and building team into a big construction company with . . . a work force of two thousand" (ibid., p. 294). In a brisk account of how he built up his enterprise, the manager said disarmingly: "As I see it, what the country's most short of now is managerial talent, not people with

Sally Stewart is Lecturer in the Department of Management Studies, University of Hong Kong, and specializes in research on the Chinese business scene. Chong Chung Him took his M.B.A. at the University of Hong Kong and is now working in California.

diplomas. Me? I reckon I'm managerial talent."

It was obviously necessary at the outset of the study to delineate what was meant by success in a managerial career. One of the anonymous reviewers of this article (to whom the authors are deeply indebted) made the important observation that career success, managerial success, and success in obtaining one's position in the company are all different in both conceptualization and practice. This article is concerned with career success, which was equated by Margerison and Kakabadse (1985) with an individual's achievement and maintenance of a top leadership position, and this definition was adopted for the present study. All those selected for interviewing had a minimum of two years' career track record at a senior level.

Light has been thrown on success, and many other aspects of working life in present-day China, by contemporary Chinese writers, and there seems no reason to doubt that the Chinese vision of career success corresponds with the Western idea, which might be simply expressed as having power, the ability to make things happen, and status and recognition. In stories by such authors as Jiang (1983), Shen (1987), and Wang (1983), the activities and ambitions of Chinese factory managers are brought to life and the snakes and ladders in their careers illustrated. A famous example of the genre is "Manager Qiao Assumes Office" (Jiang, 1983, pp. 130–179), which first appeared in 1979 and was later adapted for both radio and television. The author "has been working in a heavy machinery plant since 1958" (Jiang, 1983, back cover) and the concrete details of actual working life and relationships within the enterprise ring true, even if the characters are rather two-dimensional.

The tensions between the managers and the cadres supervising the enterprises described in the Chinese stories have been confirmed in such scholarly works as those by Laaksonen (1988), Warner (1987), and Lieberthal and Oksenberg (1988). The last drew attention to "the various bargains that upper and lower levels strike in order to advance particular initiatives" (ibid., p. 401) and pointed to the development of networks "bound by mutual obligations and patron–client ties" (ibid., p. 406) and to the fact that "administrators seek self-sufficiency. . . . They hoard information, feign compliance, cultivate patrons at higher levels" (ibid., p. 409). Chinese managers have to operate in this environment and the question is what qualities enable them to do so successfully. Little attention seems to have been paid to this issue, although the complications of negotiating with the Chinese have been extensively studied (Pye, 1982; Tung, 1982; Stewart and Keown, 1989). Specific difficulties, for example, with technology transfer to the PRC, have been described (Stewart and Keown, 1989) and some problems facing Chinese managers examined (Anzizu, in press; Fukuda, 1988).

The working lives of Western executives have been extensively studied since Carlson's (1951) study, which was followed by Stewart's (1965 and 1967) analyses of managerial work. Both these researchers used the diary method, while Mintzberg (1973) relied on structured observation of, or actually living with, the

American CEOs whose activities he described, for the data in his much-cited work.

Kotter (1982) made comprehensive observations on 15 general managers over a few years, and Norburn (1987) undertook a comparative study of 1,708 American senior vice presidents and 418 British counterparts, including an analysis of their perceptions of aspiration levels and executive success traits. Earlier, Margerison and Kakabadse (1985) carried out research, published by the American Management Association, on 711 American CEOs, focusing on the elements leading to a successful managerial career. One of the most recent analyses is probably that by Korn (1988), for which he conducted in-depth studies of 24 top company officials to attempt to discover the reasons for their career success.

While much has been published on both Western and Japanese managerial activities, a paper by Doktor, Redding, and Bidgood (1985), which examined the work activities of five ethnic Chinese CEOs in Hong Kong and contrasted their use of time with that of the American CEOs described by Mintzberg (1973), would seem to be the only attempt to date to compare ethnic Chinese and American managers' activities. However, of "the five Chinese CEOs studied, four had extensive exposure to Western education. . . . Consideration must be made for the sample's 'Westernisation'" (Doktor, Redding, and Bidgood, 1985, p. 57).

Methodology

The problems of choosing an appropriate methodology to investigate managerial behavior in the PRC have been discussed at length by Adler, Campbell, and Laurent (1989), who found that asking managers to complete questionnaires themselves was so unsatisfactory that they suggest, "items incorporating the notion of 'truth' . . . are more or less irrelevant" for Chinese managers (ibid., p. 71). The present authors had already rejected the use of written questionnaires, since, in an earlier study of thirty managers from Shanghai, these had proved unsatisfactory, almost certainly in this case because of unwillingness to commit information to paper.

It was, therefore, decided that all the research should be carried out by means of personal interviews conducted inside the PRC by one of the authors, who is a native Chinese speaker but also completely at home with the literature written in English in this field. There was, therefore, no question of language or translation difficulties, since the co-author was doing the interviewing. Those selected for interview were people with whom the co-author had in most cases a business relationship over the years and who, therefore, knew and trusted him. Questionnaires were only used to structure the interview and were completed by the interviewer rather than by the individual managers.

It was decided to confine this study solely to managers in a single modern industry (electronics), partly because of the co-author's personal knowledge and

Table 1. Profiles of those interviewed

age	no.	sex	no.
25–29	1	male	24
30–34	3	female	2
35–39	2		
40–44	10	*total interviewed*	26
45–49	4		
50–54	6		
total interviewed	26		

location of present firm	no.	level of education	no.
Beijing	8	secondary school	2
Guangzhou	3	university*	18
Shenzhen	3	postgraduate school	6
Zhuhai	2		
Shanghai	1	*total interviewed*	26
total of firms	17		

*including military academy

no. of employees in present firm*	no.	type of present firm	no.
less than 500	1	state-owned	10
500 - 1000	8	state-affiliated	5
1000 - 3000	3	independent	2
3000 - 5000	2		
Over 5000	3	*total of firms*	17
total of firms	17		

*including group organizations directly below the firm

years of service in present firm	no.	function	no.
3 years or less	2	engineering	4
3–5 years	5	sales & marketing	9
5–10 years	8	production	3
10–15 years	3	personnel	1
over 15 years	8	accounting	1
		foreign trade	5
total interviewed	26	general management	3
		total interviewed	26

experience of the Chinese electronics industry, and partly because it was felt that more valid comparisons with Western managers could be made if those studied were working in a modern, high technology field.

The major environmental differences between the working life of a Chinese manager in a rural agricultural enterprise, who might not even have easy access to a telephone, and the life of a Western manager is too great to allow meaningful comparisons. The decision to confine this study to managers in a single industry was also made as a result of the earlier attempt to study a group of thirty managers from Shanghai, which had shown the need to limit the scope of the research in order to isolate certain common characteristics. Two of the electronic businesses were owned and run independently of the state. Another five were "state-affiliated" enterprises collectively owned by private individuals; they were permitted to set their own strategies, hire and fire staff without going through the official bureaucracy, and maintain control over salaries as described by Williams (1987). Ten were state owned.

Among the problems encountered in preparing the study was that of deciding upon exactly who qualified as a "senior manager." As Handy (1985) said: "It has never been easy to define what a manager is, or what he does." The same can be said for senior executives or managers. However, while a rigorous definition is not possible, there are some managerial functions that are commonly accepted as belonging to senior managers. For example, Peters and Waterman (1982) proposed that by "senior management" was meant the group of people assuming ultimate leadership in the organization, who chart its direction, formulate the business strategies, manage (directly or indirectly) the majority of the staff, and command the allocation of the available resources. These were the criteria whereby those to be interviewed for this study were selected. Altogether a total of twenty-six senior executives from seventeen different enterprises were questioned during 1987 and 1988. A further eleven interviews with people working closely with those in the sample were conducted to ensure the reliability of the data and it was also checked against personal observation during visits to the organizations. Table 1 gives details of those interviewed.

Results

In an attempt to discover real, rather than theoretical, reasons, all managers were asked a preliminary general question about their opinions as to whether there were any key elements to which they attributed their present leadership positions. Each interviewee was asked to name and rate in descending order (with scores 5 to 1) no more than five reasons. The 26 managers ranked the key elements, which they thought had led to their success, as shown in Table 2.

It can be seen that most of the elements described relate to individual personality traits rather than to work activities, and that they are not necessarily areas on which management training can have an effect. You cannot teach someone to

Table 2. Reasons for success

ranking	element	score
1.	Interpersonal relationships: an ability to maintain harmonious relationships with all the people with whom they came in contact in their jobs	42
2.	Personal training: especially in the 3 areas of engineering, management, and foreign languages	38
3.	Hard work: willing to sacrifice personal enjoyment and leisure and give extra effort to their work	34
4.	Luck: career advancement as a result of both external and internal opportunities	33
5.	Willingness to take risks, to make personal commitments	32
6.	Proven competence	28
7.	Loyalty and seniority in the organization	26
8.	Aggressiveness: a strong desire to achieve and a determination to get to the top	19

Note: Other elements listed by a minority of interviewees included military experience, good health, family support, sincerity, patriotism, innovation, flexibility, humility and personal insight.

be lucky, however vital luck may be to a successful career. Therefore, a further set of questions was posed, relating to working activities mainly using the categories employed by Mintzberg (1973).

In order to identify elements for success based on working functions, each manager was asked which activity:

(1) he or she perceived as most important,
(2) he or she would like to devote more time to,
(3) he or she would like to spend less time on, and
(4) he or she perceived as least important.

"Activity" was defined as being something within the seven groups of functions on which the vast majority of all the manager's time was spent. The results are shown in Tables 3–6 and the following sections deal with each major activity separately.

Training

The managers perceived personal training as the most significant element in their success and wanted to spend more time on it. They made great efforts to find time to read, used tape recorders as training tools, and attended seminars.

It is worth noting that the urge of the PRC managers to learn was not due to a

Table 3. Activity perceived as most important

ranking	activity	score	%
1.	personal training	12	46
2.	scheduled meetings	8	31
3.	desk work	5	19
4.	unscheduled meetings	1	4
total		26	100

Table 5. Activity on which the manager would like to spend less time

ranking	activity	score	%
1.	scheduled meetings	14	54
2.	business trips	9	35
3.	desk work	3	11
total		26	100

Table 4. Activity on which the manager would like to spend more time

ranking	activity	score	%
1.	personal training	10	39
2.	desk work	7	27
3.	unscheduled meetings	6	23
4.	scheduled meetings	3	11
total		26	100

Table 6. Activity perceived as least important

ranking	activity	score	%
1.	local transportation	7	27
2a.	business trips	6	23
2b.	scheduled meetings	6	23
4.	unscheduled meetings	4	15
5.	desk work	3	11
total		26	100*

*rounded up from decimal places

lack of education: 24 out of the 26 managers were already well educated by Chinese standards, having completed university or equivalent courses. The urge for more training seemed to stem from rapid changes with which they found difficult to cope.

Another point related to the desire for training was that, as shown above, hard work had a high score among the general key elements considered as fundamental to career success. A manager who pursued personal training diligently was looked upon as a hard-working individual, thereby winning the respect of his supervisors and colleagues. Some interviewees cited hard work as a vital consideration in selecting their successors.

Desk work

Desk work was also perceived by the 26 managers as an essential element in their success but, by desk work, the managers meant the planning process and reading, rather than writing. When they cited desk work as the least important activity, managers had time spent on writing in mind.

Senior managers considered spending time alone at their desks to formulate strategies, analyze the environment, and speculate on the contingent scenarios vital to success. It was pointed out by one manager, who had undergone extensive training in foreign organizations, that most Chinese organizations did not have staff planners at the senior level, so that managers had to assume the planning role themselves, since, even in a planned economy, each enterprise needs to work out a program of work.

One other important aspect of desk work was reading official reports and memoranda. Most interviewees paid very close attention to any material circulated to them, including promotional mail from the outside. They regarded this type of reading as a basic duty that had to be performed effectively, not only to gain information but also to set an example to their colleagues.

Scheduled meetings

The managers had mixed feelings toward scheduled meetings. One interviewee said: "The [scheduled] meetings are important and you cannot afford to skip them, although they are so time-consuming." In other words, for senior managers the opportunity cost attached to these meetings was quite considerable, but they considered that they had to pay it.

The attitude toward scheduled meetings may be partially explained by the high value set on interpersonal relationships by the Chinese managers. A meeting might be a vehicle to acquire information or solve problems. But it could also help to develop an understanding of those who attended, and to exert influence on the others there, and indeed to signal their relationship with the others. In any case, to deal with organizational politics, a senior manager could not afford to absent himself, however much he disliked wasting time at meetings.

There was also the chance of gaining information. While the main content of the discussion might be anticipated, it was possible that some critical news might surface at the meeting. One manager said that he might have to sit in a meeting for three hours to pick up only one piece of information, but that snippet might be vital to his operations.

It was also recognized that some of the top management decisions had to be made collectively; brain storming might be necessary; and consensus and compromise needed to be reached. Meetings were essential to achieve all of these purposes. Finally, attendance at meetings was another sign of diligence, which helped to win the respect of colleagues and thus maintain leadership among the group.

Unscheduled meetings

Unscheduled meetings were also a very effective means of facilitating the flow of information. As Mintzberg (1973) found, they were much favored for this reason by Western managers, but in China the chief value of unscheduled meetings was seen in different terms.

The importance of *guanxi*, or personal connections, in China is well recognized. It has been remarked that "your position depends on whom you know," and a wide network of acquaintances helps enormously in lobbying, soliciting, negotiating, and even confronting. Most interviewees stressed the ability to develop and maintain good working relationships with colleagues and outside contacts as an important factor in their success, and stated that unscheduled meetings provided a better opportunity to cultivate valuable interpersonal relationships than formal meetings. It may also be that environmental uncertainty, for instance the frequent disruption of supplies, was the reason for many of the unscheduled meetings.

Business trips

Business trips were not popular among the 26 senior managers. The opportunity cost involved in staying away from the office was high, especially when communications were difficult, and most of the managers felt they should delegate as many trips as possible to their assistants.

However, one sales manager remarked that business trips gave him firsthand knowledge of the markets and personal contacts with key customers. Moreover, he saw his shuttles among the various cities as evidence of aggressiveness, hard work, loyalty, and commitment, which had earned him respect and accelerated his promotion.

American views on key elements in managerial success

Table 7 lists 21 key elements of significance to career development based on Margerison' and Kakabadse's (1985) survey of the perceptions of 711 chief executive officers in the United States. Key factors cited by these managers can be grouped under two headings:

(1) Leadership experience, a proven track record in a broad range of functional areas established at an early stage of one's career, and

(2) Personal factors, especially motivational drive, interpersonal skills, and communication ability.

Comparing Table 7 with Table 2, some common features in both the U.S. findings and the Chinese results can be distinguished. These include harmonious human relationships, personal training, a propensity to take risks, a career track record, and a need to achieve. However, the importance ascribed to each point was significantly different. Not surprisingly, interpersonal relationships were perceived as of high importance by both the PRC and the Western managers, and it may reasonably be assumed that this is a fundamental requirement for successful managers throughout the world. However, the significance of on-going personal training was given more weight in China, whereas a strong need to achieve results, a sound track record (leadership experience), and a high propensity to take risks were all rated much higher in the United States than in China.

**Table 7. Margerison and Kakabadse's 1985 rating of the impact of
21 key elements on career development in the United States**

1.   A need to achieve results
2.   An ability to work easily with a wide range of people
3.   Challenge
4.   A willingness to take risks
5.   Early overall responsibility for important tasks
6.   A width of experience in many functions prior to the age of 35
7.   A desire to seek new opportunities
8.   Leadership experience early in one's career
9.   An ability to develop more ideas than other colleagues
10a. An ability to change one's managerial style to suit the occasion
10b. A basic desire to determine the central strategy of an organization according to
     one's own principles
12. A determination to get to the top, ahead of others
13. An ability to make "deals" and negotiate
14. A sound technical training
15. Family support (parents/spouse)
16. Visibility to top management before the age of 30
17. Developing and using political skills in the organization
18. A manager early in one's career who acted as one's model
19. Special "off-the-job" management training
20. An experience of leadership in the armed forces
21. Changing jobs at regular intervals

Four factors listed by the PRC managers were missing from the Americans'
21 key elements—hard work, luck, loyalty, and seniority—but it must be re-
membered that, as with the definition of managerial activity, the perception of
the elements leading to managerial success was subjective. The Western managers might have taken for granted that hard work, loyalty, and seniority were
prerequisites for success, as suggested in Margerison and Kakabadse's (1985)
report, but the Chinese managers saw these qualities as being worthy of special
mention. There may be cultural reasons why American executives are reluctant
to ascribe their success to "luck": it may hint at a degree of fatalism not felt
acceptable in the American system.

Conclusions

This study suggested, not surprisingly, that both the Chinese and American managers identified certain similar elements as contributing to managerial success.
However, there were also some marked differences in the factors singled out by
the two groups. The PRC senior managers felt that personal training and development were the most important factors in career success. Although they worked

as long hours as, or even longer hours than, their American counterparts, they did not put much emphasis on it. Korn's (1988) survey found that the average American corporate chief put in 56 hours a week at the office and 49 days a year on the road, while, on the average, Chinese managers interviewed for this study claimed to work 11.7 hours a day, 6 full days a week, and to spend about 15 percent of their time (3.9 weeks a year) away from their home base. Those interviewed for the Korn (1988) survey attributed their success to hard work and suggested that their lives revolved around their work and that they were prepared, if necessary, to sacrifice family life for their careers. Little evidence of such a conflict appeared with the Chinese managers, and this might be worth researching in the future.

It may also be worth noting in passing that "high personal intelligence was thought vital to succeed in Britain, whereas in America intelligence achieved the penultimate lowest rank" (Norburn, 1987, p. 26) and it was not mentioned at all by the Chinese managers, who thought interpersonal relationships, hard work, competence, and commitment and loyalty to the organization were the best ways to earn respect and trust.

It seems reasonable to assume that, after forty years of socialism, a Chinese manager will prefer collective decision making and to have his orders endorsed, rather than run the risk of being accused at some future date of resorting to Chairman Mao's (1967) great sin of "commandism," and this may be one of the reasons for their stress on the importance of getting on with people. Moreover, managers in China need to maintain a network of personal contacts in order for the enterprise to obtain the resources to be able to function.

It is interesting to speculate whether the Chinese managers' emphasis on further training was due to the fact that none had any formal business education, whereas Norburn (1987) found that 45 percent of both U.S. and British managers in his study held MBA degrees.

The current interest in management education in the PRC, described by Hildebrandt and Liu (1988), reflects this Chinese desire for further training, and it is to be hoped that this article may help those involved. Kirkbride, Tang, and Shae (1989) specifically mention the need "for much more research on the day to day activities of Hong Kong managers and an in-culture identification of skill deficiencies and development needs" (ibid., p. 13). This would seem to be equally needed for China's managers.

References

Adler, J.; Campbell, N.; and Laurent, A. (1989) "In Search of Appropriate Methodology: From Outside the People's Republic of China Looking In." *Journal of International Business Studies*, Spring, pp. 61–74.

Anzizu, J. M. de. (in press) "General Management in China: An Emerging and Complex Task." In S. Plasschaert and N. Campbell, eds., *The Changing Nature of Management in China*, Part 1, chapter 5. London: JAI Press.

Carlson, S. (1951) *Executive Behaviour: A Study of the Work Load and the Working Methods of Managing Directors*. Stockholm: Strombergs.

Doktor, R. H.; Redding, S. G.; and Bidgood, J. (1985) "Hong Kong and American C.E.O.s: Are They Oceans Apart in Their Use of Time?" *Hong Kong Journal of Business Management*, III, pp. 57–62.

Fukuda, K. J. (1988) "Chinese Management: Whatever Happened to its Traditions?" Appendix to *Japanese-style Management Transferred*. London: Routledge.

Handy, C. B. (1985) *Understanding Organizations*. England: Hazell Watson & Viney.

Hilderbrandt, H. W., and Liu, Jinyun. (1988) "Career and Education Patterns of Chinese Managers." *The China Business Review*, November/December, pp. 36–38.

Jiang Zilong. (1983) *All the Colours of the Rainbow* (translated by Wang Mingjie). Beijing: Chinese Literature Press, Panda Books.

Kirkbride, P. S.; Tang, S. F. Y.; and Shae Wan Chow (1989) "The Transferability of Management Training and Development: The Case of Hong Kong." *Asian Pacific Human Resources Management*, February, pp. 7–19.

Korn, L. (1988) *The Success Profile*. New York: Korn-Ferry International.

Kotter, J. P. (1982) *The General Managers*. New York: Free Press.

Laaksonen, O. (1988) *Management in China during and after Mao in Enterprises, Government, and Party*. Berlin and New York: Walter De Gruyter.

Lieberthal, K., and Oksenberg, M. (1988) *Policy Making in China: Leaders, Structures, and Processes*. Princeton, NJ: Princeton University Press.

Mao Tse-Tung (1967) *Quotations*. Beijing: East is Red Publishing House, p. 287.

Margerison, C., and Kakabadse, A. (1985) *How American Chief Executives Succeed*. New York: American Management Association.

Mintzberg, H. (1973) *The Nature of Managerial Work*. New York: Harper & Row.

Norburn, D. (1987) "Corporate Leaders in Britain and America: A Cross-National Analysis." *Journal of International Business Studies*, Fall, pp. 15–32.

Peters, T. J., and Waterman, R. W., Jr. (1982) *In Search of Excellence*. New York: Harper & Row.

Pye, L. W. (1982) *Chinese Commercial Negotiating Style*. Cambridge, MA: Oelgeschlager, Gunn & Hain.

Shen Rong. (1987) *At Middle Age* (in translation). Beijing: Chinese Literature Press, Panda Books.

Stewart, R. (1965) "The Use of Diaries to Study Managers' Jobs." *The Journal of Management Studies*, 2, pp. 228–235.

———. (1967) *Managers and Their Jobs*. London: Macmillan.

Stewart, S. (1988) "The Transfer of High Technology to China: Problems and Options." *International Journal of Technology Management*, 3 (1/2), pp. 167–179.

Stewart, S., and Keown, C. F. (1989) "Talking with the Dragon: Negotiating in the People's Republic of China." *Columbia Journal of World Business*, 24 (3), Fall, pp. 68–72.

Tung, R. L. (1982) "U.S.–China Trade Negotiations: Practices, Procedures and Outcomes." *Journal of International Business Studies*, 13, pp. 25–28.

Wang Meng. (1983) *The Butterfly and Other Stories* (in translation). Beijing: Chinese Literature Press, Panda Books.

Warner, M. (ed.) (1987) *Management Reforms in China*. London: Frances Pinter (Publishers).

Williams, F. E. (1987) "The Emergence of Entrepreneurship in China." Working Paper. Houston, TX: Rice University.

Zhang, Xin-Xin, and Sang, Ye. (1986) *Chinese Profiles* (in translation). Beijing: Chinese Literature Press, Panda Books.

CHRISTINE NIELSEN SPECTER
AND JANET STERN SOLOMON

The Human Resource Factor in Chinese Management Reform

Comparing the Attitudes and Motivations
of Future Managers in Shanghai, China;
Baltimore, Maryland; and Miami, Florida

Introduction

The winds of change are blowing in the People's Republic of China (PRC) as state leaders consider either accepting or rejecting Western business principles and practices as necessary components of economic growth. The move toward the acceptance of Western business principles could be traced to December 1978, when Deng Xiaoping, at a meeting of the Central Committee of the Communist Party, called for an increased role for the market, liberalization of thought, and strengthening of democracy and the legal system. According to the Central Committee, no country could progress if it refused to accept elements of advanced science and culture from abroad (Schram, 1987). Coincident with this change in the macro environment, far-reaching management reforms were being undertaken to assure that economic principles were translated into business practices. A leading example is Rong Yiren, a communist bureaucrat, who was handpicked by Deng in 1980 to serve as chairman of China International Trust and Investment Corporation. CITIC was involved with many aspects of domestic business activity and had a virtual franchise on overseas investment. What were the concepts that Rong associated with business success? He applauded entrepreneurial activity, aggressive and creative individuals who are not afraid to make mistakes, and organization structures that provide incentives to these individuals, while not restricting them with unnecessary bureaucracy (Kraar, 1987). Many experts believe that Chinese managers must be trained in light of these concepts

The authors are at the Department of Management and International Business, Florida International University, Miami, FL, and the Department of Management, Towson State University, Towson, MD, respectively.

if Western business principles and practices are to play a positive role in the PRC's economic development.

Certain studies suggest that managerial talents are broad, human qualities transcending cultural differences (Ghiselli, 1971; Haire, Ghiselli, and Porter, 1966; Hofstede, 1972), and that individuals who lack these vital managerial characteristics can change their attitudes and behaviors through appropriate education and training (McFie, 1961; Farmer and Richman, 1965). In line with this philosophy, China is importing management education from the West, increasing ties with colleges of business in the United States. An example of this strategy is the National Center for Industrial Science and Technology Management Development in Dalian. Three programs offered include a six-month course for enterprise managers, a six-week version for senior executives, and an MBA program, called the Young Executives Program. The programs are partly funded by the U.S. Department of Commerce and are taught by U.S. instructors, through the State University of New York at Buffalo (Kempe, 1986). The purpose of the program is to import "foreign" concepts, including competition, acceptance of failure, focus on the "bottom line," and motivational theories.

Purpose

Given this significant interest in the traits and behaviors of Western managers, in 1988 the authors surveyed upper-level undergraduate business students in Shanghai, China; Baltimore, Maryland; and Miami, Florida in order to provide a descriptive comparison of their abilities, traits, and motivations in certain areas considered critical to managerial success. In comparative management research today, the question is being asked whether or not the nation-state can be used as the unit of analysis in cross-cultural studies (Ronen, 1986). For example, some studies indicate that a percentage of differences in attitudes, characteristics, and perceived needs can be linked to nationality. Haire, Ghiselli, and Porter (1966) reported that the percentage of difference in managerial job attitude attributed to nationality is 28 percent; Hofstede (1980) found that national culture explained 50 percent of the differences in employee attitudes and behaviors. At the same time, neither educators nor researchers should assume a homogeneous group of U.S. students, inculcated with Western business values, when conducting cross-national comparisons. Neither should they assume that a group of students from one area in China is representative of that nation as a whole. With these constraints in mind, the authors undertook this research to provide a comparison of undergraduate business students from Shanghai with students from two distinct locations in the United States: Baltimore and Miami. The authors sought to avoid facile descriptions of any of these three groups that might suggest they were representative of national cultures.

The purpose of this research is twofold. First, it provides information that may be considered by policy makers and educators as they train the next generation of Chinese business leaders and enterprise managers, those who will be responsible for translating far-reaching management reforms into practical business applications. An understanding of similarities and differences among business students in these two societies is a necessary foundation for the educational planning process. With this knowledge, programs are more likely to be designed to meet critical needs. Second, this study provides information that should be considered by cross-cultural researchers who frequently base their conclusions on comparisons of national cultures. This study examines whether or not this is appropriate in terms of studies related to transferring Western business attitudes to China. The authors focused their attention on six factors: achievement, intelligence, self-assurance, decisiveness, initiative, and risk-taking ability, which are discussed in more detail in the literature review below.

Six factors indicative of managerial success

Murray (1938) and more recently McClelland (1961) and Atkinson (1964) have proposed that a good deal of an individual's will to perform can be explained by the strengths of various personality-need variables. These needs channel and regulate the flow of potential energy. Americans tend to see themselves as individuals while, in many other countries, people see themselves as part of a group (Butterfield, 1982). Thus, definitions of "success" may differ, with Americans defining success in personal terms and other cultures defining success in family terms. To investigate this possibility, England and Lee (1974) examined the relationship between managerial values and managerial success for a sample of American, Australian, Indian, and Japanese managers. Results indicated that the relationship between personal values and success were rather similar among managers from the four countries. Thus, it may be possible to look at managerial success and related managerial traits and motivations in terms that extend beyond national or cultural confines.

The need for achievement, defined as the drive to excel, to achieve in relation to a set of standards, to strive to succeed, has been the target of much research. McClelland (1961) found that high achievers seek situations where they are personally responsible for finding solutions to problems, where they receive clear feedback on their performance to know whether they are improving or not, and where they can set moderately challenging goals. According to McClelland, managers seek the challenge of working out problems and accepting responsibility for success or failure. It has been shown that high achievers are successful in entrepreneurial activities such as operating their own businesses, or managing self-contained units within a large organization (McClelland and Winter, 1969). Furthermore, employees can be successfully trained to stimulate their achievement needs (Miron and McClelland, 1979).

A number of cross-cultural studies have examined differences and similarities in achievement needs (Ajiferuke and Boddewyn, 1970; England and Lee, 1974;

Gruenfeld and MacEachron, 1975; Hines and Wellington, 1974; Hofstede, 1976; Sirota and Greenwood, 1971). Several studies have dealt with the achievement needs of the Chinese (McClelland, 1963; Shenkar and Ronen, 1987). Devos (1968) observed that the Chinese achieve considerable economic success, even though the culture has been traditionally characterized as having a low achievement need (Bhagat and McQuaid, 1982).

While level of intelligence has been linked to managerial level and to successful performance (Miner, 1973; Ghiselli, 1971; Heller and Porter, 1966), no information was uncovered that related level of intelligence to managerial performance in China.

The ability to take risks has been linked to managerial success (Ghiselli, 1971; Miner, 1985). Numerous cross-cultural studies have addressed this relationship, looking at the risk-taking ability and the mirror image of security needs (England, Dhingra, and Agarwal, 1974; England and Lee, 1974; Gruenfeld and MacEachron, 1975; Hofstede, 1976; Ronen and Kraut, 1977). Little research has been conducted on the needs of Chinese for security, but one study comparing security needs of Hong Kong Chinese and Westerners revealed a far greater security need among the Chinese (Redding, 1980). Several studies point to a strong concern among Chinese managers for material security, with money serving as a symbol of security (Chui, 1977; Lemming, 1977; Nevis, 1983; Silin, 1976).

Research findings indicate that risk-taking ability is positively correlated with self-assurance (Clausen, 1965; Burnstein, 1969). Self-assurance is a quality that separates those managers who see themselves as captains of industry from those who see themselves as mere cogs in the organizational machinery (Ghiselli, 1971). However, no cross-cultural studies have considered this trait in relation to managerial performance in China.

Decisiveness is important for all managers, whether in small businesses or vast organizations. Mintzberg (1973) observed four decisional roles that executives perform; in all four of these roles, decisiveness is necessary for a successful manager. One well-known cross-cultural study focused on decisiveness (Hofstede, 1976). Bass and Burger (1979) studied the relative speed of decision making among managers in various countries. A mere handful of studies have looked at this quality among Asian managers (Moddie, 1970; Sethi, 1973; Long and Seo, 1977), while no studies have appeared linking decisiveness and managerial performance in China.

Similarly, initiative is necessary for managers to move the organization forward and maintain a competitive position. Individual initiative influences both the advancement of the person (achievement needs) as well as of the organization (Ghiselli, 1971). Haire, Ghiselli and Porter (1966) conducted a cross-national study that examined linkages between initiative and management practices. This study did include results from Asia, but none for Chinese managers.

This literature review reveals that very little has been written about Chinese managers from the People's Republic of China in terms of the six factors discussed above. Few comparative management studies focus on any Asian countries other than Japan (Adler, Doktor, and Redding, 1986). In their review of the literature, the authors found no research that attempted to look at the traits and motivations of future business leaders in China in order to assess their capacity to accept and carry out Western business principles in the Chinese environment. For this reason, the authors compared Chinese and U.S. business students in relation to the six factors (achievement, self-description of intelligence, self-assurance, decisiveness, initiative and risk-taking ability) using a survey instrument, the Ghiselli Self-Description Inventory (SDI) described below.

The authors hypothesized that: (1) there would be no significant differences between the two groups of U.S. students related to their scores on the six factors; (2) the U.S. students would be similar to managers in terms of their mean scores; (3) there would be no significant differences among the three groups on the self-description of intelligence scale, and (4) there would be significant differences between the mean scores of the Chinese students and each of the two U.S. groups on the remaining five scales, with U.S. students scoring higher than their Chinese counterparts on the four traits positively linked to managerial success and lower on the need for security scale, which is negatively correlated to managerial success.

Methodology

The sample population for this study included 150 upper-level undergraduate business students from Shanghai University of Technology, Shanghai, PRC; Towson State University, in a suburb of Baltimore, Maryland, and Florida International University, Miami, Florida. Students participated in this study by filling out the Ghiselli Self-Description Inventory (SDI).

The purpose of the instrument is to measure individual and group scores associated with nine traits linked to managerial success (Ghiselli, 1971). Six of the nine traits were those identified by the authors in the previous section: need for occupational achievement, intelligence, self-assurance, decisiveness, need for security (as indicative of risk-taking ability), and initiative. Three additional traits (supervisory ability, self-actualization, and lack of working-class affinity) were recognized by Ghiselli's study. Supervisory ability may mean something significantly different in the organizational context of the PRC than in the United States, however. Self-actualization is also viewed differently in an individualistic culture such as the United States, than in a group-oriented society such as the PRC. Given the historical background of the PRC, one cannot assume that lack of working-class affinity would be positively regarded by Chinese managers. Thus, these three traits were excluded in this comparison.

SDI was chosen from a number of alternative tests that cover one or more of the six traits in which the authors were interested. In the selection process, the authors considered the number of traits covered by the instrument, reports concerning the instrument's reliability and validity (Frederiksen, Jensen, and Beaton, 1972; Brief, Aldag, and Chacko, 1977; Miner, 1978), the length of time required to take the test, and the relative ease of translating this instrument into Chinese. The SDI included all six characteristics. Each was represented on the instrument by a series of paired, personally descriptive adjectives of similar social desirability. The use of such adjectives was in keeping with guidelines that have been presented in the literature concerning the writing of test materials in English that are readily translatable and have the best chance of representing core meanings of the included items across cultures (Brislin, 1986).

Ghiselli constructed each of the measurement scales by selecting two criterion groups in the United States, one consisting of individuals high in a given trait; another consisting of individuals low in that trait. Next, the two groups took a paired-adjectives test. Only those items to which the two groups responded significantly differently were included on the scale. Finally, the test was administered to over 300 U.S. managers (approximately half of whom had been evaluated as successful and half as less successful by their superiors) to identify the relative importance of these traits to managerial success.

This discussion of instrument design raises the issue of the appropriateness of using an instrument developed in one country as a basis for cross-cultural comparison. On the positive side, the conservation of time and expense associated with designing a new instrument or with modifying an existing instrument is a major consideration. Also, use of a recognized instrument like the SDI allows the researchers and those who follow to tie in to an existing literature concerning a set of commonly shared concepts and definitions.

However, a major criticism of this approach could be that scales drawn up in one culture, based on omission of those items low on item-to-total correlation, theoretically leaves a set of "purified items" for measuring the characteristic under consideration. Yet this may not represent the best set of items for representation of the characteristic in another cultural environment (Brislin, 1986, p. 145). In this case, the items selected would represent a less than optimal set for discrimination between those high in the characteristic from those low in the characteristic within the foreign culture. The highest scores in the foreign culture would tend to be lower than in the culture within which the instrument was designed, leading to a regression toward the mean. Since the purpose of the research is to examine the relative standing of the domestic culture vis-à-vis the foreign culture, the results would imply that the foreign sample is lower in the characteristic, when actually the lower mean score is an artifact of the instrument design. Also, the relationships discovered between these characteristics and managerial success may be quite different in a foreign environment from that found in the country in which the test was created.

These problems suggest that the design of a new instrument, developed through a similar set of processes as the SDI but normed in China, should be considered as an alternative to the current method. However, in addition to the time and money that this procedure would have required, there is a substantive issue that precludes this approach. First, the SDI scales were developed using groups of approximately 100 people who were high on the characteristic and another 100 who were low on the characteristic. These groups had been identified as being high (or low) in areas such as risk taking, initiative, self-assurance, etc. It would be difficult to identify samples of sufficient size for this portion of the design, since the Chinese sources one might approach for the samples have not been describing or evaluating individuals along these lines. Second, Ghiselli was able to administer the test to over 300 U.S. managers to ascertain which of the identified characteristics were related to managerial success. At this stage of Chinese management reform, it would be difficult, if not impossible, to find a similar sample of managers who have been identified by their superiors as successful or unsuccessful in the application of Western business principles and practices in China.

An alternative recommendation would be to modify the existing test items to assure that the terms used represent shared, core meanings between the two cultures. The use of careful translation by a recognized language expert is one approach to dealing with the modification issue, since this should reduce the probability that the included items will represent different meanings in the two cultures. In addition, back translation is used in the decentering process to assure that the language in which the instrument was created is not the center of attention. If a concept survives the decentering procedure, it is assumed to be etic, i.e., representative of a common meaning across the cultures under investigation (Brislin, 1986, pp.159–163; Longabaugh, 1980, pp. 103–104).

The Shanghai students in our study completed the questionnaire in Chinese. The SDI was translated into Chinese and translated back into English by the Berlitz Translation Service. In this way, we responded to the instrument modification issue.

Results

Data analysis began with a calculation of the mean responses of the three student groups for each of the six traits. These mean scores were compared. Likewise, the mean scores of the three groups were compared with the mean scores of managers as reported by Ghiselli (1971). The results reveal an interesting pattern (see Table 1). On the five trait scales positively related to managerial success (i.e., need for occupational achievement, self-description of intelligence, self-assurance, decisiveness, and initiative), Shanghai students hold the lowest mean scores. As expected, the Chinese students have the greatest need for security (lesser ability to take risks). Baltimore students hold the second lowest mean scores on the five traits positively linked to managerial success. This group's mean score on the need for security scale indicates that they are less risk averse

Table 1.   A comparison of business students from Miami, Baltimore, and Shanghai with managers

means and standard deviations on six scales

Group	occupational achievement (mean/sd)	self-described intelligence (mean/sd)	self-assurance (mean/sd)	decisiveness (mean/sd)	need for security (mean/sd)	initiative (mean/sd)
Managers*	41.8/8.65	41.61/7.57	28.30/5.85	22.23/4.85	10.26/3.61	32.86/6.
Miami	36.6/8.1	41.4/6.4	27.2/4.7	21.6/4.1	10.1/3.8	31.2/5.9
Baltimore	33.6/9.3	37.9/6.9	24.8/4.4	20.7/4.9	11.5/3.6	29.5/5.6
Shanghai	29.7/9.0	36.9/6.2	22.5/4.2	16.9/3.5	13.1/4.0	26.3/6.4 ·

*Source of data on managers: Edwin E. Ghiselli, *Explorations in Managerial Talent.* Pacific Palisades, CA: Goodyear Publishing Company, 1971, p. 148.

Table 2.   A comparison of business students from Miami, Baltimore, and Shanghai

Tukey's test: groups indicated below are significantly different at the 0.05 level

scale test pair	occupational achievement	self-described intelligence	self-assurance	decisiveness	need for security	initiative
Miami/ Shanghai	Miami Shanghai	Miami Shanghai	Miami Shanghai	Miami Shanghai	Miami Shanghai	Miami Shanghai
Miami/ Baltimore	Miami Baltimore	Miami Baltimore				
Shanghai/ Baltimore				Shanghai Baltimore		

than the Chinese, but have a stronger need for security than the Miami group. Finally, of the three groups of students, the Miami students hold the highest mean scores on the scales positively related to managerial success, and this group has the lowest mean score on the need for security scale, indicating that this group of students is more likely to take risks.

In comparing the student scores with Ghiselli's group of managers, the Miami student group's performance comes closest on all six scales to that of the managers. As a matter of fact, on the need for security scale, the Miami students scored slightly lower than managers.

The next step in our analysis was to determine significant differences among the mean scores of the three student groups (see Table 2). A general linear models procedure was deemed appropriate, since there was some difference in group size. (The number of usable responses in the Miami group ranged from 56 to 61, while the number in the Shanghai group ranged from 36 to 39, and Baltimore from 34 to 35.) On all six trait scales, the Miami student group response was significantly different from the Shanghai group at the 0.05 level, using Tukey's standardized range test. Miami and Baltimore students were significantly different in relation to self-perception of intelligence and self-assurance. Most surprisingly, Shanghai and Baltimore students were significantly different on only one of the six scales, decisiveness.

In summary, our original hypotheses were supported by the results to the extent that (1) Miami students' mean scores were significantly different from Shanghai scores on scales related to occupational achievement needs, self-assurance, decisiveness, need for security, and initiative, and (2) U.S. students from both Miami and Baltimore scored higher than their Chinese counterparts on the four traits positively linked to managerial success and lower on the need for security scale, which is negatively correlated to managerial success. However, we were surprised to find that (1) there were significant differences between the Miami and Baltimore student groups on two of the six scales (self-description of intelligence and self-assurance); (2) the Miami students were most similar to managers, while Baltimore students lagged in second place in terms of their mean scores; (3) there were significant differences between Miami and Shanghai, and between Miami and Baltimore on the perceived intelligence scale; and (4) no significant differences were found between Baltimore and Shanghai students on scales related to occupational achievement needs, self-assurance, need for security, and initiative.

Discussion

The lack of statistical differences between the Baltimore and Shanghai groups should prove instructive to those researchers who use national culture as a unit of analysis in cross-cultural studies. Particularly, investigators should proceed with caution in comparative studies when using a U.S. sample as representative of Western business attitudes. The Baltimore and the Shanghai students have some similarities in their backgrounds. Both Baltimore and Shanghai are port cities with numerous manufacturing operations. Both universities attract most of their students from the immediate geographic areas, with relatively few students from other states or provinces (Office of Institutional Research, 1989; Shen, 1989). Their students are mostly from families that have lived in their respective cities for many generations. In addition, students in both universities are often the first in their families to seek higher education, and the families recognize the great opportunities for advancement that college entrance represents.

In general, these conditions may explain the lack of statistically significant differences in the students' perceptions of their own initiative, self-assurance, achievement, and security needs. Looking at security needs, we can point out that most students, both in Baltimore and Shanghai, have little expectation of pursuing graduate studies. They anticipate employment, usually at large organizations, immediately following graduation. Such organizations represent security and well-defined career paths. In terms of achievement needs, Ghiselli points out that lower-level managers are valued insofar as they perform the tasks prescribed (Ghiselli, 1971, p. 81). High achievement needs could actually interfere with success in these lower-level positions. Lower achievement needs by Baltimore and Shanghai students may be in keeping with their perceived roles as lower-level managers in large organizations. Both Shanghai and Baltimore students face major obstacles in gaining college education. For the Chinese student, the major obstacle is the admissions process, due to the fact that there are college placements available for less than 4 percent of all Chinese students. Those who do attend, however, receive ample government support. On the other hand, sufficient openings do exist in the U.S. education system, but far less government assistance is available to those who aspire to obtain a college education. The ability of both groups to overcome their respective obstacles may suggest similar levels of initiative. The SDI results support this conclusion.

A major difference between the Baltimore and Shanghai students is the process by which they arrive at the university level. The Chinese government retains control over the decision to continue on to higher education or to enter the workforce. By contrast, Baltimore students have independently made the decision to take college entrance exams, complete applications, pay tuition, and forego full-time employment. This is symbolic of an environmental difference between China and the United States. Individuals in the United States are free to make more decisions related to life goals. Individual decision making is more prevalent in the United States, and this difference may explain why Baltimore students demonstrate greater decisiveness than those in Shanghai.

Another surprising finding in the study is the degree to which Miami students stand out, suggesting that of the three groups, Miami students have the greatest potential to become successful managers. What is it about the Miami students that leads them to exhibit a profile most similar to managers and least similar to Shanghai students? Miami is a center of international trade and finance, especially with Latin America. However, Shanghai is no stranger to the international arena. Shanghai businesses sell Swiss watches, Japanese cameras, and Chinese stereos, not only in Chinese currency but also in U.S. dollars. Perhaps it is its cultural diversity that differentiates the Miami environment. Florida International University students are drawn from a much wider geographic area. Only 55 percent of the student respondents were born in the United States, so that Miami represents a dynamic, heterogeneous mix of cultures in comparison to Baltimore and Shanghai. A cultural determinant of the significantly different profile may be the large number of Hispanic students in the Miami sample (62 percent). Latin cultures and their impact on student traits cannot be overlooked. The revitalization of Miami is often linked to the immigration of a large Cuban population with strong business backgrounds and entrepreneurial motivation. Over 14 percent of the Miami undergraduates were born in Cuba (38.7 percent of the Miami participants indicated their mothers were born in Cuba, and 41.9 percent indicated their fathers were born in Cuba).

Despite these unexpected results, the study supports the accepted position that Chinese students are less likely to exhibit certain characteristics than their U.S. counterparts, in terms of their ability to take risks, to be motivated by occupational achievement, to exhibit self-assurance and initiative. One explanation for these results would be that the Chinese sample exhibits a lower mean score due to the fact that the test was designed and normed in the United States (the rationale for this argument was explained in the methodology section). However, it is instructive to note that there were substantial, if not significant, differences in the mean scores of the two U.S. samples as well. The higher mean score of the two U.S. samples was always the Miami group. Since almost half of the Miami respondents were foreign born, this allows us to argue against a lower foreign-response bias.

More needs to be done to explain results related to the self-description of intelligence scale. It was hypothesized that there would be no significant differences among the student groups on this scale. Yet, scores for Miami/Shanghai and Miami/Baltimore were significantly different. The authors cannot explain these differences. Since the scale involves self-perception, these results could be related to differences in self-assurance, rather than differences in intelligence. It is possible that the Chinese participants, socialized in a collectivist culture, may tend to be more modest than the U.S. participants, socialized in an individualist culture. The ancient Chinese proverb "In that great sea a lone man drowned" could be compared to the U.S. proverb "Blow your own horn." Then, to the extent that the paired adjectives on the questionnaire were *not* "neutral" in this regard, one might expect that the Chinese would respond in a more modest fashion, achieving lower scores. However, a careful review of the items suggests that the pairings were carefully created to avoid one choice being more desirable than the other. This approach should have removed the potential of a modesty bias. Even on the self-description of intelligence scale, pairs such as friendly vs. cheerful do not seem to include this bias. However, one item on this scale may point to such a problem: enterprising vs. intelligent. For example, only 48 percent of the Chinese sample identified themselves as intelligent, while 66 percent of the Miami sample identified themselves as intelligent. It could be argued that the Chinese respondents were simply more modest about their level of intelligence. However, out of 36 items included on the intelligence scale, this was the only one that dealt directly with intelligence; the remainder were indirect and appeared relatively neutral in desirability, even across cultures.

To the extent that risk-taking ability, occupational achievement motivation, self-assurance, and initiative can be linked to managerial success within the context of the PRC environment, these results support educational programs currently underway to facilitate their acceptance by Chinese students. This information suggests that educators and policy makers, charged with the responsibility of providing society with a future generation of managers who can implement difficult managerial reforms, are on the right track, in terms of importing Western business attitudes that are in line with Western business practices. The differences between the Chinese and the U.S. students' scores may suggest to educators and policy makers that more needs to be done in terms of programs aimed at attitudinal change. Perhaps model programs underway in certain cities should be undertaken by educational institutions in other parts of China. These results point to one area that could receive further attention. The authors are not aware of programs that are specifically aimed at increasing the students' self-confidence or self-assurance. This may be an area that should be explored especially, since it is tied to risk-taking ability.

The results of this research provide a descriptive comparison of Chinese business students from one area of the PRC with students from two distinctly different environments in the United States. However, many questions are left unanswered. Considering studies of broader scope, it would be interesting to expand the study in terms of the original three groups, or to compare these findings with similar studies involving other U.S. regions and other regions in China. We argued in the methodology section that, in 1989, Chinese management reform was not sufficiently advanced to consider designing a new instrument based on characteristic scales created within the Chinese environment, and keyed to those characteristics of managerial success necessary to apply Western business principles and practices within the Chinese context. However, sometime during the next five years, this might be an attractive undertaking. It would be very interesting to compare the results obtained from such an instrument with that of the SDI. Also, the present study could be enlarged to consider how business students from other cultures or countries would perform on the SDI instrument. The dynamics of the Miami situation could be explored in much greater detail, in order to compare Hispanic scores to non-Hispanic scores, and Cuban scores to other Hispanic groups.

Looking toward the future

A *Wall Street Journal* article in February 1989 proclaimed that China appears irreversibly launched on the road to modernization, calling China a "college classroom on capitalism" (House, 1989). Major issues must be resolved if economic reforms are to be implemented in China, particularly given the post Tiananmen Square environment. Whatever the future holds, the road ahead will not be a smooth one. Many of the students who have been educated within the framework of Western business attitudes and practices are finding it difficult to apply these concepts within their organizations, battling tough resistance from bureaucrats clinging to the old ways (Leung, 1988).

The ultimate responsibility for the organizational transformations that lie ahead rests with today's college students, because they are the business leaders and enterprise managers of tomorrow. As we contemplate the challenges ahead, their attitudes and motivations cannot be overlooked. Hopefully, this research has contributed to a better understanding of this significant group.

Acknowledgments

The authors express their appreciation for the research assistance provided by Rosana Coloma, Elizabeth Cross, Diane Perry-Rojas, and Robert Prieto, at Florida International University. The assistance of the Faculty Research Committee of Towson State University is gratefully acknowledged.

References

Adler, N. J.; Doktor, R.; and Redding, S. Gordon. (1986) "From the Atlantic to the Pacific Century: Cross-Cultural Management Revisited." *Journal of Management*, 12 (2), p. 307.

Ajiferuke, B., and Boddewyn, J. (1970) "Culture and Other Explanatory Variables in Comparative Management Studies." *Academy of Management Journal*, 13, pp. 153–165.

Atkinson, J. W. (1964) *An Introduction to Motivation*. Princeton, NJ: Van Nostrand.

Bass, B. M., and Burger, P. C. (1979) *Assessment of Managers: An International Comparison*. New York: Free Press, 1979.

Bhagat, R. S., and McQuaid, S. J. (1982) "The Role of Subjective Culture in Organizations: A Review and Direction for Future Research." *Journal of Applied Psychology Monograph*, 67 (5), pp. 635–685.

Brief, A. P.; Aldag, R. J.; and Chacko, T. I. (1977) "The Miner/Sentence Completion Scale: An Appraisal." *Academy of Management Journal*, 20, pp. 635–643.

Brislin, R. W. (1986) "The Wording and Translation of Research Instruments." In *Field Methods in Cross-Cultural Research*, vol. 8. Cross Cultural Research and Methodology Series, pp. 137-164. Edited by W. J. Lonner and J. W. Berry. Beverly Hills: Sage Publications.

Burnstein, E. (1969) "An Analysis of Group Decision Involving Risk." *Human Relations*, 22, pp. 381–395.

Butterfield, F. (1982) *China: Alive in the Bitter Sea*. New York: Bantam Books.

Chui, V. C. L. (1977) Managerial Beliefs of Hong Kong Managers. Unpublished master's thesis, University of Hong Kong.

Clausen, G. (1965) Risk Taking in Small Groups. Doctoral dissertation, University of Michigan, Ann Arbor.

Devos, G. A. (1968) "Achievement and Innovation in Culture and Personality." In *The Study of Personality: An Interdisciplinary Approach*, E. Norbeck, D. Price-Williams, and W. M. McCords, eds. New York: Holt, Rinehart and Winston.

England, G. W.; Dhingra, O. P.; and Agarwal, N. C. (1974) *The Manager and the Man*. Kent, OH: Kent State University Press.

England, G. W., and Lee, R. (1974) "The Relationship between Managerial Values and

Managerial Success in the United States, Japan, India, and Australia." *Journal of Applied Psychology*, 59 (4), p. 411.

Farmer, R. N., and Richman, B. M. (1965) *Comparative Management and Economic Progress*. Homewood, IL: Irwin.

Fredericksen, M.; Jensen, O.; and Beaton, A. E. (1972) *Predictions of Organizational Behavior*. New York: Pergamon.

Ghiselli, Edwin E. (1971) *Explorations in Managerial Talent*. Pacific Palisades, CA: Goodyear Publishing Company.

Gruenfeld, L. W., and MacEachron, A. E. (1975) "A Cross National Study of Cognitive Style among Managers and Technicians." *International Journal of Psychology*, 10 (1), pp. 27–55.

Haire, M.; Ghiselli, E. E.; and Porter, L. W. (1966) *Managerial Thinking: An International Study*. New York: John Wiley and Sons.

Heller, F. A., and Porter, L. W. (1966) "Perceptions of Managerial Needs and Skills in Two National Samples." *Occupational Psychology*, 40, pp. 1–13.

Hines, G. H., and Wellington, V. U. (1974) "Achievement and Motivational Levels of Immigrants in New Zealand." *Journal of Cross-Cultural Psychology*, 5, pp. 37–47.

Hofstede, G. (1972) "The Color of Collars." *Columbia Journal of World Business*, September/October, pp. 72–80.

_____. (1976) "Nationality and Espoused Values of Managers." *Journal of Applied Psychology*, 61 (2), pp. 148–155.

_____. (1980) *Culture's Consequences: International Differences in Work Related Values*. Beverly Hills: Sage.

House, K. E. (1989) "Communist Giants Are Too Burdened at Home to Lead Much Abroad." *Wall Street Journal*, 6 February, pp. 1, 4.

Kempe, F. (1986) "Executives of China's State-Owned Firms Learn to Do Business the American Way." *Wall Street Journal*, 19 February.

Kraar, L. (1987) "China's Mister Right." *Fortune*, 5 January, p. 109.

Kraut, A. I., and Ronen, S. (1975) "Validity of Job Facet Importance: A Multinational Multicriteria Study." *Journal of Applied Psychology*, 60 (6), pp. 671–677.

Lemming, F. (1977) *Street Studies in Hong Kong*. Hong Kong: Oxford University Press.

Leung, J. (1988) "Chinese M.B.A. Holders Find a Degree Earned in West Doesn't Go Far at Home." *Wall Street Journal*, 2 June, p. 18.

Long, A. W., and Seo, K. K. (1977) "Epilogue: Contrasts in Management Practices." *Management in Japan and India*, 16, p. 260.

Longabaugh, R. (1980) "The Systematic Observation of Behavior in Naturalistic Settings." In *Handbook of Cross-Cultural Psychology*, H. C. Triandis and J. W. Berry, eds., pp. 57–126. Boston: Allyn and Bacon, Inc.

McClelland, D. C. (1961) *The Achieving Society*. Princeton, NJ: Van Nostrand Reinhold.

_____. (1963) "Motivational Patterns in Southeast Asia with Special Reference to the Chinese Case." *Journal of Social Issues*, 19 (1), pp. 6–19.

McClelland, D. C., and Winter, D. G. (1969) *Motivating Economic Achievement*. New York: Free Press.

McFie, J. (1961) "The Effects of Education on African Performance on a Group of Intellectual Tests." *British Journal of Educational Psychology*, 31, pp. 232–240.

Miner, J. B. (1973) *Intelligence in the United States*. Westport, CT: Greenwood Press.

_____. (1978) "The Miner Sentence Completion Scale: A Reappraisal." *Academy of Management Journal*, 21, pp. 283-294.

_____. (1985) *The Practice of Management*. Columbus, OH: Charles E. Merrill Publishing Co.

Mintzberg, H. (1973) *The Nature of Managerial Work*. New York: Harper & Row.

Miron, D., and McClelland, D. C. (1979) "The Impact of Achievement Motivation Training on Small Business." *California Management Review*, pp. 13-28.

Moddie, A. D. (1970) "The Making of an Indian Executive." *Indian Management*, 9 (8) (August), p. 45.

Murray, H. A. (1938) *Explorations in Personality*. New York: Oxford University Press.

Nevis, E. C. (1983) "Cultural Assumptions and Productivity: The United States and China." *Sloan Management Review*, 24 (3), pp. 17-28.

Office of Institutional Research. (1989) "Towson State University Enrollment Summary." University Report, 9 (unnumbered pages).

Redding, S. G. (1980) "Cognition as an Aspect of Culture and its Relation to Management Processes: An Exploratory View of the Chinese Case." *Journal of Management Studies*, 5, p. 136.

Ronen, S. (1986) *Comparative and Multinational Management*. New York: John Wiley and Sons.

Ronen, S., and Kraut, A. I. (1977) "Similarities among Countries Based on Employee Work Values and Attitudes." *Columbia Journal of World Business*, 12, pp. 89-96.

Schram, Stuart. (1987) "Deng's Decade." *The World in 1987*, p. 40.

Sethi, N. (1973) "The Japanese Managerial Scene: An Introductory View." *Marquette Business Review*, Winter, p. 203.

Shen, Yikang. (1989) Telephone interview with the Deputy Dean, Economic Management School and Chairman, Industrial Foreign Trade Department, Shanghai University of Technology, November.

Shenkar, O., and Ronen, S. (1987) "Structure and Importance of Work Goals among Managers in the People's Republic of China." *Academy of Management Journal*, 30 (3), pp. 564-579.

Silin, R. H. (1976) *Leadership and Values: The Organization of Large Scale Taiwanese Enterprises*. Cambridge, MA: Harvard University Press.

Siroka, D., and Greenwood, J. M. (1971) "Understanding Your Overseas Workforce." *Harvard Business Review*, 49 (1), pp. 52–60.

MICHAEL MINOR AND B. CURTIS HAMM

The "Little Dragons" as Role Models

Management Implications for China

China is too often analyzed without regard to the example of other developing countries. A discussion of development models suggests that China's situation can fruitfully be analyzed as similar to that of the four "Little Dragons" (Taiwan, South Korea, Singapore, and Hong Kong), and to Japan in an earlier era. Because of the unusual size of Hong Kong and Singapore, and the special political status of Hong Kong, most attention is focused on China, Taiwan, and South Korea. Various implications for management and the external environment for management are discussed.

Introduction

Beginnning in 1978, China engaged in a massive reorientation of her economy, which has been characterized by paramount leader Deng Xiaoping as China's "Second Revolution." The primary themes of the reforms were to diminish the role of state planning, enhance the autonomy of enterprises, increase competition among business entities, and provide direct economic incentives for improved performance to both enterprises and employers. The domestic reforms were complemented by a significant effort to integrate China's economy with the international economic system.

Given these changes, it is not very useful to analyze China in terms of the "Maoist" model of development. China has effectively rejected wholesale the fabric of that model, despite the events of the summer of 1989, which point to a political retrenchment even while many of the economic reforms remain in place. China's recent reforms must be understood in a comparative perspective.

Post 1978 China can be analyzed better by using models from political economy. This approach is useful because China's economic opening to the rest of the world needs to be addressed, and the political economy literature directly ties countries into the international economy. There are two dominant models of

The authors are Associate Professor of Marketing and International Business at the University of Texas–Pan American, Edinburg, TX, and Norick Brothers Distinguished Professor of Marketing, Oklahoma City University, Oklahoma City, OK, respectively.

political economy and a third incipient model. We argue that the third model is more fruitful in developing propositions that reflect China's current level of development and help to describe the environment for Chinese management policy in the immediate future.

The two dominant international political economy models are dependency theory and developmental theory (see, for example, Biersteker, 1978; Jackman, 1982; Stephen, 1978; Clark and Chan, 1990; and Chan, 1987). The following sections summarize the main tenets of each model.

The developmentalist model

Developmentalists are the intellectual heirs of Adam Smith and David Ricardo, and hence supporters of free trade. Economically, developmentalists stress the importance of domestic factors in the economy and the "spirit of enterprise." Developmentalists advise active participation in the international economy, which will lead to the benefits of economic specialization. All nations will enjoy the fruits of producing in economic sectors where they have a comparative advantage. Socially, developmentalists believe that natural economic processes will promote growth if the social barriers inherent in "traditional societies" are removed. Politically, while government intervention is necessary from time to time to achieve public purposes, the role of the state is best restricted to as little interference in the economy as possible.

In sum, the developmentalist perspective is fundamentally optimistic about prospects for development. The operation of market forces will promote development. The political and social factors that affect the operation of markets are central variables. The developmental perspective focuses on domestic decisions that promote development.

The dependency model

The dependency model follows a different line of reasoning. Economically, dependency theory emphasizes external factors. The economies of Third World countries are initially integrated into the international economy as sources of raw materials. This division of labor is perpetuated by the power of the developed world. The international division of labor has been most clearly associated with Wallerstein (1979), who characterizes these relationships as core–periphery relations. For Wallerstein, the industrialized core exploits the underdeveloped periphery. This division of labor causes serious distortions in the economies of developing countries. One example of these distortions is the domination of the developing country's economy by foreign multinational corporations. Socially and politically, the economic and political elites in peripheral states form alliances with their counterparts in developed countries. This draws their attention away from the development needs of their own countries, and toward a value system and lifestyle appropriate to the core, developed nations.

In sum, dependency theory is at bottom pessimistic about the development prospects of underdeveloped nations. The structure of the world economy conditions economic growth. The limits to growth are based on macrostructural factors, and are therefore largely beyond the ability of the underdeveloped state to control.

A third model

Neither the developmental nor the dependency models pays much attention to the role of the state in promoting development. Recently a new perspective has evolved that is more state-focused.

A major advocate of this perspective is Bruce Cumings (1984a), who applies this approach to Meiji Japan, South Korea, and Taiwan. Cumings calls this application of a state-centric focus to Asian countries the "BAIR," or bureaucratic–authoritarian industrializing regime, model. Some of the more important characteristics of a BAIR include:

1. relative state autonomy: the state is not simply reflective of the demands and interests of groups within the state;
2. central coordination;
3. authoritarian regimes;
4. bureaucratic short- and long-range planning; and
5. high flexibility in moving in and out of economic sectors.

This model can usefully be applied to Singapore and Hong Kong (and perhaps Malaysia and Thailand: see Clark and Chan, 1990) as well as Japan during modernization in the Meiji era, Taiwan, and South Korea. However, Singapore and Hong Kong are difficult to compare with other countries: are they countries? city-states? Further, their small size has dictated an orientation toward light manufacturing and entrepot-area activities, conditions that do not obtain for China or the other areas. Therefore, attention will be directed primarily to Taiwan and South Korea as exemplars of the BAIR development model and their possible relevance as harbingers of future developments in China.

China's Second Revolution

Before applying the BAIR approach to China's contemporary economic policies, a few words are in order about the evolution of China's development strategy. In the first decade after the founding of the PRC, China stressed economic autarchy, even though China engaged in trade and technology transfer with the Soviet Union, and followed the Stalinist emphasis on building heavy industry through centralized planning (Ray, 1975). Generally, however, China's economic policy was based on self-reliance.

This policy of self-reliance was accompanied by a series of economic upswings and wrenching setbacks. Periods of relative economic prosperity, such as during the first five-year plan in the mid 1950s and the period under Liu Shaoqi from 1961 to 1965, were followed by periods of economic reversal, for example, during the disastrous Great Leap Forward in the late 1950s and the Cultural Revolution in the late 1960s.

The command economy and policy of self-sufficiency created a number of problems. Among them were the stifling of initiative of enterprise management, inefficient resource allocation, and the lack of work incentives. The Cultural Revolution, in particular, wasted human capital in terms of dislocation and missed educational opportunities.

As a response, in 1978 Deng Xiaoping set China's "Second Revolution" in motion. Under the "four modernizations" (in agriculture, industry, defense, and science and technology), Deng directed that China was to be modernized through revitalized industry and agriculture. The four modernizations have led to a wide variety of innovations. The range of reforms is extensive. For example, China established a stock market in the late 1980s, although activity was never vigorous and has recently slowed to a crawl (Ignatius, 1988, 1990a). China even has a new bankruptcy law to handle the demise of inefficient enterprises (Minor and Stevens-Minor, 1988).

When Zhao Ziyang, former chairman of China's Communist Party, visited the Xiamen Special Economic Zone, he urged that officials help reduce the state's role in the economy. Two weeks later, city planners auctioned off three state-owned, money-losing enterprises to the highest bidder. Auctions in Fujian province were even opened to foreign bidders.

Externally, China's modernization was to be aided through an "open door" toward international trade and investment. The open door marked a change of great scope from China's former policies toward the rest of the world. The policy of self-reliance was emphatically reversed. As Zou Siyi of the PRC Export Bureau said in 1979: "There is no such thing as a completely autarchic country. Furthermore, there is no country that became modernized by closing its doors" (Cumings, 1984b).

Specifically, the open door policy emphasized two new policy directions: (1) increasing trade, especially with the West; and (2) attracting foreign investment to China.

Foreign trade

China became an active participant in world trade in the post 1978 period. Chinese foreign trade languished at the level of $2 billion in 1952, increasing only to $4.3 billion in 1965. But it reached $20.6 billion by 1978, more than doubled again by 1984, and continued to grow in the latter 1980s. China enjoyed a trade surplus from 1980 to 1983, and foreign reserves rose from $2.3 billion to $14.3 billion during that period.

In 1984, however, China posted a trade deficit of $9.5 billion, and the deficit climbed to $12 billion in 1986 before dropping to $3.7 billion in 1987. China had

**Table 1. China's foreign trade
selected years, 1952–1987**

year	total amount*
1952	2.0
1957	3.1
1965	4.3
1978	20.6
1984	49.8
1985	59.2
1987	64.0

*In billions of U.S. dollars

Sources: Rabushka (1987); Frankenstein (1986); various issues of *The Economist* and *The Wall Street Journal.*

resorted to strong state intervention, restricting imports and increasing export incentives to decrease the deficit. By the end of the 1980s, however, China's trade deficit was once again rising. China has consistently run trade deficits with its largest trading partner, Japan, although its trade surplus with the United States has nearly tripled from $2.1 billion for 1986 to $6 billion in 1989, and may be as high as $11 billion in 1990 (*The Economist*, May 1990). China's foreign exchange reserves reflected her trade performance, dropping from a peak of $17 billion in July 1984 to only $11.9 billion at the end of 1985, although reserves have rebounded to $14 billion in 1990 (Taiwan, in contrast, had $44 billion in reserves in 1986 and $70 billion in 1990). Thus, while great strides have been made in the expansion of foreign trade, China's performance pales in comparison with Taiwan and South Korea, both of whom engaged in foreign trade at nearly twice the rate of China in the late 1980s.

Foreign investment

In 1979 Fujian and Guangdong provinces were authorized to set up Special Economic Zones (SEZs) to attract foreign investment. Guangdong established three SEZs in Shenzen, Zhuhai, and Shantou, while Fujian set up a zone in Xiamen. In 1984, fourteen more cities were opened for foreign investment. These zones were modeled on export-processing zones in other developing countries (including Taiwan) and were intended to replicate the freewheeling economic environment of Hong Kong. In the zones, the Chinese government provided infrastructure and reduced taxes and customs duties. Managerial discretion was granted to foreign owners.

On balance, China's foreign investment program has been modestly successful at best. Over 2,300 joint venture proposals were written from 1979 to 1985, and there were over 1,300 proposals in 1985 alone. However, most of these proposals have remained on the drawing board, actual capital commitments have been small, and many of them are offshore-oil exploration contracts or tiny textile and electronic-assembly equity ventures from Hong Kong and Macao (Clary and Liu, 1987; Beamish and Wang, 1989; *The Wall Street Journal*, 1989). Only the Shenzhen SEZ has operated without significant problems. Located close to Hong Kong, Shenzhen has provided a good marriage between Hong Kong's capital, technology, and entrepreneurial know-how and Shenzhen's land and manual labor. Even in Shenzhen, however, only 20 percent or so of the manufactured products leaving Shenzhen have actually been exported, with the rest entering the Chinese domestic market (Rabushka, 1987). Further, the relatively meager benefits of foreign investment have largely remained limited to the coastal areas near the zones and to large cities such as Beijing and Shanghai (Barnard and Shenkar, 1990). In other words, the Chinese have committed to allowing foreign investors into China, but have not succeeded in fostering a foreign investment climate that serves China's development goals.[1]

A reexamination

The results of China's economic innovations since 1978 can be viewed in terms of two factors: (1) China's place in the international product life cycle, and (2) the role of the state in promoting development.

As to China's place in the international product life cycle, China is clearly following the example of the "Four Dragons," particularly Taiwan and South Korea, as these countries move from labor-intensive light industry to more sophisticated capital-, skill-, and technology-intensive products. Taiwan and South Korea are themselves receptacles for declining Japanese industries, as the Japanese move on to more technically advanced products. The textile industry is a convenient example: Japan was once a major supplier of textiles to the United States, but this industry migrated to Taiwan and Korea as Japanese labor costs rose. In turn, China is now a major supplier of textiles to the United States, as labor costs have driven management in Taiwan and South Korea to seek opportunities in more upstream areas such as electronics and automobile production.

In terms of the role of the state in promoting development, China relies upon central coordination despite the increasing autonomy of business enterprises. The government sponsors and directs the country's fundamental structural changes in the economy. State enterprises continue to play an important role in the economy. For example, in 1985 some 70 percent of urban industrial output was the product of state-owned enterprises (Rabushka, 1987), although private enterprises are the fastest-growing segment of Chinese industry, averaging production growth rates of 80 percent per year between 1980 and 1986.

Classifying China

If we return to the three models of development mentioned earlier, China does not fit the dependency model, because she has been at pains to integrate herself into the world economy at a rapid pace. On the other hand, China's government is clearly interventionist vis-à-vis the economy, and thus does not fit the developmentalist model.

China does appear to fit relatively easily into the parameters of the bureau-cratic–authoritarian industrializing regime model. To coin a rather bad phrase, the Chinese dragon becomes a BAIR. Here it should be noted that in China an interventionist state government engages in central coordination and planning. This regime is authoritarian, as the events of June 1989 vividly demonstrate. A central bureaucracy attempts to plan and manage economic development, even while attempting at the same time to capture the benefits of the marketplace. Thus one can perhaps speak of a continuum of regime types, anchored at one end by liberal–democratic states and at the other by totalitarian states. Taiwan and South Korea occupy a roughly middle position, with China (and certainly East-ern Europe, perhaps even the Soviet Union) moving at various rates of speed toward the center.

The applicability of the BAIR model as exemplified by Taiwan and South Korea is shown by the increasing role of foreign trade in the Chinese economy. China's exports are already at roughly the level of Taiwan and South Korea. There is, of course, not the same level of dependence on trade at present: foreign trade represents 91 percent of Taiwan's GNP, and 86 percent of South Korea's. The trajectory of China's trade growth, however, shows a similarity among the three countries. China's foreign trade doubled as a percentage of national income between 1981 and 1985, and while in 1985 foreign trade represented only 13 percent of the national income (Frankenstein, 1986), by 1990 foreign trade repre-sented a third of national income (*The Economist*, June 1990).

Also, Deng's well-known efforts at decentralization of the economy prior to the summer of 1989 represent an attempt to inject a measure of the economic magic of Taiwan and South Korea into China, using similar tools of liberalized foreign-investment regimes, less central planning, export-led growth, and the like. In the future, of course, China will have to determine whether to follow the Taiwan variant of smaller, more entrepreneurial firms, or to adopt the Korean model of larger conglomerates, a pattern that closely follows the Japanese model of industrial concentration (*The Economist*, July 1990). This decentralization effort has been stymied in the post-Tienanmen period, of course, and it will not be nearly enough to put decentralization back on the agenda in a formal sense: the next time management must feel reasonably confident that the reforms will stick. It remains to be seen how this confidence can be obtained.

Cumings's other criterion for a bureaucratic–authoritarian industrializing re-gime—high flexibility in moving in and out of economic sectors—is not yet evident in China. But this is precisely what Deng tried to achieve by allowing private enterprise to establish itself. In the next few years, provided that the decentralization of management and the role of private enterprise resume, this enterprise flexibility may also appear. At the same time, it should be noted that Chinese hardliners and economic-planning bureaucrats have reversed, at least temporarily, the role of private enterprise as an engine of economic growth.

Conclusion

Finally, we should ask what insights into the future we might gain from applying the bureaucratic–authoritarian industrializing regime model to China. Can meaningful propositions be developed? A few examples would include the following.

Politically, it would not be far-fetched to suggest that China in twenty years may bear some resemblance to Taiwan and South Korea, although the events of June 1989 make this forecast problematic. As with Taiwan and South Korea, a significant element of state ownership of economic enterprises would still exist. This might include state ownership of banking and heavy industry, as well as possibly other sectors over which the Chinese government wishes to maintain direct control, as well as the provision of infrastructure by the state. China's rate of development would not compare with that of Taiwan and South Korea, of course. However, it is at least possible that in the future, discussion of trade and investment may include references to "China, Inc." as well as "Korea, Inc." and "Japan, Inc." As with Taiwan and South Korea, direction by Chinese political institutions may allow the state to pursue successful policies and structural transformations.

At the same time, the examples of Taiwan and South Korea suggest that economic growth produces a momentum toward liberalization and democratization. We were beginning to see this in the PRC until 1989, and we may very well see it again in the future.

China's adoption of a model of development similar to that of Taiwan and South Korea also poses a possible problem. If the strategy of export-led growth is generalized, this could lead to a flood of exports that would outrun the political capacity of the advanced industrial societies to absorb them. In other words, export-led growth can be practiced successfully by only a few states at a time. China may find herself increasingly excluded from the lucrative markets of the West as her export capabilities grow. In fact, pressures from other export-led developers, as well as the increasing exports of Western Europe that are likely after unification in 1992, may push the United States and Europe toward protectionist policies at a rate faster than China's own export growth would appear to demand. China could easily become a victim of other nations' successes. This would force Chinese managers to cast about for an alternative model—an unpleasant prospect, because the import-substitution model has proven much less profitable.

One is tempted to speculate as well about whether a larger market composed of the "China markets" (the PRC, Taiwan, Hong Kong, and Singapore) could evolve over time. The close link between the PRC and Hong Kong economies is well known, and there is a Taiwan–PRC economic connection as well. Taiwan is experiencing the effects of economic success: labor shortages, a strong currency that drives export prices upward, and a vocal environmental lobby. Taiwan businessmen have backed some 1,000 projects in China worth about $1 billion, and trade between Taiwan and the mainland reached $3.8 billion in 1989, up 28 percent from the year before. In the first six months of 1990, Taiwanese investments in Fujian province were double the dollar amount of the same period in 1989. Singapore has less involvement with the PRC, which is a major source of Singapore's imports but not a large market for exports. Hong Kong and the PRC will almost certainly continue to grow closer economically on the way to the reversion of Hong Kong in 1997. Indeed, China can arguably be viewed as a vast labor pool that could be harnessed by Hong Kong, Taiwan, and Singapore businesspeople who share the language and culture of their mainland brethren (Ignatius, 1990b).

Managerially, the foregoing discussion suggests a number of implications. First, models of management with potential application to China are available by studying management in Taiwan and South Korea, since they are both examples of the BAIR pattern. Further, their general cultural similarity, notwithstanding clear differences between the Chinese and the Koreans, makes the models of Taiwan and South Korea particularly suited to serve as analytic foci.[2]

Second, the role of state planning will hinder the ability of enterprises to develop their own system of ordering, inventory control, pricing of scarce resources, and even distribution. Greater freedom to plan from the enterprise position is required for growth.

Third, competition should still increase on a domestic basis as enterprises see internal possibilities for growth. However, international competition will be increasingly difficult as incomes inside China improve and the Pacific Rim countries accelerate their managerial expertise.

Fourth, performance improvement of managers and employees is critical if enterprises are to compete externally. External consultants have shown their effectiveness, but have perhaps not been utilized as much as is appropriate. Change in this area will require greater incentives (probably in the financial area) to provide rewards for improvements.

Fifth, prior to June 1989, China's climate for enterprise provided an environment under which managers could develop the leadership and education to bring enterprises to higher levels of performance and competition. However, the BAIR model clearly indicates that the transition would have been difficult prior to the government's 1989 crackdown. It is clearly impossible until the momentum that had developed prior to 1989 is regained.

Finally, at the level of strategic management, political events have overtaken the usual strategic considerations of which management must take heed. One is reminded of Mintzberg's (1988, 1989) distinction between deliberate and emergent strategy. In China, it can be said that deliberate strategy can be formulated only when the political tea leaves are read and their meaning digested; and emergent strategy evolves in response to the evolving political situation.

Notes

1. A more detailed investigation is provided in Engholm (1989). For assessments after the June 1989 suppression of the pro-democracy movement, see Ignatius (1989); *The Economist* (May 1990); and Worthy (1990).

2. In fact, a good deal of writing has pointed to the general cultural similarity among China, Japan, Korea, Taiwan, Singapore, and Hong Kong stemming from the shared "Confucian ethic," and the possible implications for development of this similarity. See Kahn (1979); Berger and Hsiao (1988); Hofstede and Bond (1988); and Clark and Chan (1990). An explanation of growth in East Asia that does not rely on cultural factors is provided in Chan (1987).

References

Barnard, Mark, and Shenkar, Oded. (1990) "Variations in the Economic Development of China's Provinces: An Exploratory Look." *GeoJournal*, 21, May/June, pp. 177–183.

Beamish, Paul W., and Wang, Hui Y. (1989) "Investing in China via Joint Ventures." *Management International Review*, 1, pp. 57–64.

Berger, Peter L., and Hsiao, H. M. M., eds. (1988) *In Search of an East Asian Development Model*. New Brunswick, NJ: Transaction Books.

Biersteker, Thomas J. (1978) *Distortion or Development? Contending Perspectives on the Multinational Corporation*. Cambridge, MA: MIT Press.

Chan, Steve. (1987) "Comparative Performances of East Asian and Latin American NICS." *Pacific Focus*, Spring, pp. 35–56.

"China: Smiling Away the Tienanmen Blood." (1990) *The Economist* (June 2), 34-36.

Clark, Cal, and Chan, Steve, eds. (1990) "Special Issue: The East Asian Development Model." *International Studies Notes*, Winter.

Clary, John M., and Liu, Xianfeng. (1987) "Rough Ride on a New Road: The AMC Joint Venture in China." Paper presented at the Annual Meeting of the Academy of International Business, Chicago.

Cline, William R. (1982), "Can the East Asian Model of Development Be Generalized?" *World Development*, 10, February, pp. 81–90.

Cumings, Bruce. (1984a) "The Origins and Development of the Northeast Asian Political Economy: Industrial Sectors, Product Cycles, and Political Consequences." *International Organization*, 38, Winter, pp. 1–40.

_____. (1984b) "The Political Economy of China's Turn Outward." In Samuel S. Kim, ed., *China and the World*. Boulder, CO: Westview Press.

Engholm, Christopher. (1989) *The China Venture: America's Corporate Encounter with the People's Republic of China*. Glenview, IL: Scott, Foresman.

"Foreign Investors Shudder Over China: Ventures Are Put on Hold Pending Outcome of Nation's Struggle." (1989) *The Wall Street Journal* (June 6), A23.

Frankenstein, John. (1986) "Understanding Chinese Trade." *Current History*, September, pp. 249–270.

Hofstede, Geert, and Bond, Michael Harris. (1988) "The Confucius Connection: From Cultural Roots to Economic Growth." *Organizational Dynamics,* 16, Spring, pp. 5–21.

"If Saying it with Flowers Didn't Work, Try Cold Water" (1990), *The Economist* (May 19), 25-26.

Ignatius, Adi. (1988) "China Stock Owners Aren't Exactly Sure What Stock Is for." *The Wall Street Journal*, February 9, p. 41.

_____. (1989) "Wariness About Business in China Persists." *The Wall Street Journal*, June 15, p. A11.

_____. (1990a) "For Chinese Speculators, the Streets Offer Better Deals Than the Stock Exchange." *The Wall Street Journal*, July 6, p. A4.

_____. (1990b) "Going Home: China's Old Enemies, Capitalist Taiwanese, Now Invest in Mainland." *The Wall Street Journal*, August 2, pp. A1–A8.

Jackman, Robert W. (1982) "Dependence on Foreign Investment and Economic Growth in the Third World." *World Politics*, 34, Spring, pp. 175–196.

Kahn, Herman. (1979) *World Economic Development: 1979 and Beyond*. Boulder, CO: Westview Press.

Minor, Michael, and Stevens-Minor, Karen J. (1988) "China's Emerging Bankruptcy Law." *The International Lawyer*, 22, Winter, pp. 1217–1226.

Mintzberg, Henry. (1988) "Opening Up the Definition of Strategy." In James Brian Quinn, Henry Mintzberg and Robert N. James, *The Strategy Process: Concepts, Contexts, and Cases*. Englewood Cliffs, NJ: Prentice-Hall, Inc.

_____. (1989) *Mintzberg on Management: Inside Our Strange World of Organizations*. New York: The Free Press.

Rabushka, Alvin T. (1987) *The New China: Comparative Economic Development in Mainland China, Taiwan, and Hong Kong*. San Francisco: Pacific Research Institute for Public Policy.

Ray, Dennis M. (1975) "Chinese Perceptions of Social Imperialism and Economic Dependence: The Impact of Soviet Aid." In Bryant G. Garth, ed., *China's Changing Role in the World Economy*. New York: Praeger.

Stephen, Alfred. (1978) *The State and Society: Peru in Comparative Perspective*. Princeton, NJ: Princeton University Press.

"Taiwan and Korea: Two Paths to Prosperity" (1990), *The Economist* (July 14), 19-22.

Wallerstein, Immanuel. (1979) *The Capitalist World Economy*. Cambridge, England: Cambridge University Press.

Worthy, Ford S. (1989), "Doing Business in China Now." *Fortune* (Pacific Rim 1989 report), pp. 21–32.

PART TWO

FOREIGN AFFILIATES AND TRADE

Mary B. Teagarden
and Mary Ann Von Glinow

Sino–Foreign Strategic Alliance Types and Related Operating Characteristics

Implications for Research and Practice

Introduction

The reality of foreign business operations in the People's Republic of China (PRC) is challenging foreign investors and Chinese alike. Barely a decade ago, as part of massive economic reform, China's doors were cautiously cracked open to the West after an extended period of isolation. The doors have remained open, but the form and degree of foreign investment and involvement in China remain a controversy. Some Chinese prefer less foreign involvement than others, and a small but growing segment even prefer the wholly foreign-owned enterprises.

Despite their preference for wholly owned subsidiaries (WOSs), most transnational corporations (TNCs) engage in some form of strategic business alliance with Chinese enterprises or the government, although the WOS category is growing. These Sino–foreign alliances include (1) equity joint ventures; (2) contractual joint ventures; (3) process/assembly-buyback agreements; (4) long-term licensing agreements; (5) dynamic technology transfer agreements; (6) compensation trade agreements—including counter-trade and counter-purchase; and, (7) exploration and research consortia.

While reduction of risk, economies of scale, vertical quasi integration, and overcoming government-mandated investment and trade barriers are all identified as motivations for the use of alliances (Beamish, 1985; Contractor and Lorange, 1988), Teagarden (1990) found that the perception of government mandate was the primary motivator for alliance formation in a sample of sixty-seven

The authors are at the Department of Management, College of Business Administration, San Diego State University, San Diego, CA, and the Department of Management and Organization, Graduate School of Business Administration, University of Southern California, Los Angeles, CA, respectively.

Table 1. Proportions of foreign investments in the PRC, 1979–1986

investment form	number of contracts		value of commitment	
	U.S.	all foreign	U.S.	all foreign
equity joint ventures	72.0%	41.3%	12.2%	20.6%
contractual joint ventures	17.4%	56.4%	40.9%	49.3%
oil exploration consortia	8.2%	0.5%	44.1%	16.7%
wholly foreign-owned affiliates	2.3%	1.8%	0.2%	3.1%
compensation trade	***	***	2.6%	7.5%
other	***	***	***	2.9%

Note: Due to rounding off, percentages do not add up to 100%.

Source: Adopted from *U.S. Joint Ventures in China: A Progress Report.* National Council for U.S.–China Trade, 1987.

manufacturing equity and contractual joint ventures in the PRC.

Inherent in the use of alliances are control, autonomy, and other trade-offs that WOSs commonly do not make, a comparison that has been discussed in the literature (Contractor and Lorange, 1988; Killing, 1983). However, there has been little attention given to the nature of these trade-offs among different alliance types. The following discussion identifies four types of alliances and discusses trade-offs in operational characteristics among the types. Management of these trade-offs presents challenges to both Chinese and foreign partners (Von Glinow and Teagarden, 1988; Schnepp et al., 1990), and understanding both the types and related operating characteristic variations are a necessary starting point for meeting these challenges.

The incidence of Sino–foreign strategic alliances

The preponderance, by far, of foreign businesses operating in the PRC are engaged in some form of business alliance, business arrangements where the partners exchange some degree of operating autonomy, decision-making control, and strategic flexibility enjoyed in WOSs for other benefits. All foreign investors combined had 97 percent of their capital commitments in the PRC in alliances, with an aggregate value of U.S.$ 15.7 billion in 1987 (National Council, 1987; Yue, 1987). As of 1987, Hong Kong had 63.8 percent, the United States had 13.1 percent and Japan had 9.8 percent of the foreign capital commitments in the PRC.

The proportional differences in the use of alliance types among foreign countries investing in the PRC is shown in Table 1; for example, American TNCs invest in equity joint ventures almost twice as often as other foreign investors. However, all investors use alliances much more often than the usage rate generally encountered in international business. For U.S.-based companies worldwide, alliances outnumber WOSs four to one. However, over two-thirds of the value of this U.S. foreign investment is done through WOSs (Contractor and Lorange,

1988, p. 4). This pattern of TNC investment in the PRC varies significantly from the overall pattern of cooperative alliances in international business, and is attributed primarily to PRC foreign investment policies (Teagarden, 1990).

A Sino–foreign strategic alliance typology

The Chinese have entered into various alliances with foreign firms. While many of these alliances have been loosely identified by the Chinese and others as "joint ventures," they represent the seven investment modes identified above. These various modes can be categorized into four types that differ significantly in operational characteristics. The following discussion presents an alliance typology, and provides examples for each of the four types. These types are then used as the basis for contrasting operational characteristics.

Alliances can be differentiated based on two dimensions: an *obligation* dimension and an *involvement* dimension. The obligation dimension, which is either reciprocally based or contractually based, defines the profit allocation structure and the extent of rights and other obligations. The involvement dimension, defined as operating or passive, reflects the degree of partner interdependence and locus of decision making. The operating or passive nature of partner involvement determines operational characteristics, including the degree of strategic flexibility, the degree of operating autonomy, the level of alliance-related decision-making control, and is associated with the level of outcome uncertainty encountered in alliances. The obligation and involvement dimensions can be combined to identify four types of strategic alliances, shown with examples in Figure 1. Once the types are identified, operational characteristic trade-offs can be differentiated, as shown in Figure 2 and discussed below.

The obligation dimension

The profit allocation structure, and the extent of rights and other obligations, are essentially reciprocity schemes. In strategic alliances, these have traditionally been distinguished as having either an equity or a contractual base (Beamish and Banks, 1987; Harrigan, 1985a; Wang, 1984; Wright, 1981). In *equity-based alliances*, reciprocity is explicitly defined as an even exchange, since benefits received from the alliance are directly proportional to the contributions made to the alliance. In equity joint ventures, profit or benefit allocation (and usually decision-making control) are distributed in accordance with equity shares. This concept of explicit reciprocity can be extended to include any alliance in which the parties extract benefit from the alliance in direct proportion to their contribution to that alliance. For example, in a process/assembly and buyback agreement, the parents would not share ownership—a criterion of equity joint ventures—but the parent would receive products or services from the alliance of a value equivalent to the amount the parent invested in technology, training, and equipment.

PARTNER OBLIGATION

```
                          RECIPROCAL            CONTRACTUAL
                     |--------------------|--------------------|
                     |- EVEN EXCHANGE     |- ASYMMETRICAL      |
                     |                    |  EXCHANGE          |
                     |- PROXIMATE         |- DEFERRED          |
                  O  |  RECIPROCITY       |  RECIPROCITY       |
                  P  |                    |                    |
                  E  |     (ORAs)         |     (OCAs)         |
                  R  |--------------------|--------------------|
                  A  |     EQUITY         |    CONTRACTUAL     |
                  T  |  JOINT VENTURES    |  JOINT VENTURES    |
                  I  |                    |                    |
                  N  | Beijing Jeep Co.   | Concise Encyclo-   |
                  G  |                    | pedia Britannica   |
                     | Foxboro-Shanghai   |                    |
        I            | Company            | McDonnell Douglas  |
        N            |                    | Jet Coproduction   |
        V            | Parker-Hubei       |                    |
   P    O            | Seals Company      | Occidental Antai-  |
   A    L            |                    | bao coal project   |
   R    V            |--------------------|--------------------|
   T    E            |     (PRAs)         |     (PCAs)         |
   N    M            |                    |                    |
   E    E            | COUNTERPURCHASE &  | OIL EXPLORATION    |
   R    N            | COUNTERTRADE       | CONSORTIA          |
        T            |                    |                    |
             P       | PROCESS/ASSEMBLY-  | RESEARCH           |
             A       | BUYBACK AGREEMENTS | CONSORTIA          |
             S       |                    |                    |
             S       | DYNAMIC TECHNOLOGY |                    |
             I       | TRANSFERS          |                    |
             V       |                    |                    |
             E       | LONG-TERM          |                    |
                     | LICENSING          |                    |
                     |                    |                    |
                     |--------------------|--------------------|
```

Note: For a more detailed discussion of these types and related examples, see Teagarden and Von Glinow (1988) and Teagarden (1990).

Figure 1. A Sino–foreign business alliance typology

We refer to the obligation mode in explicit reciprocal alliances—equity and all other even-exchange relationships—as *reciprocal.*

By contrast, in *contractual or non-equity alliances*, reciprocity is merely implied. In these alliances, profit distribution structure and other rights and obligations are negotiated and embodied in a contract, not necessarily in proportion to contribution (Beamish and Banks, 1987; Campbell, 1985; National Council, 1987; Wang, 1984; Wright, 1981). Contractual alliances do not negate the expectation of reciprocal benefits: reciprocity may appear asymmetrical to the value of a partner's contribution to the alliance, when in fact expectations of reciprocity may simply be deferred. This has been observed in Sino–foreign coproduction (joint manufacturing) agreements where there is an expectation of cementing *future* business relationships through the establishment of a presence in China, thereby amounting to a deferred benefit. We identify the obligation mode in these implicit or deferred reciprocity alliances as *contractual.*

The involvement dimension

The involvement dimension differentiates alliances as either operating or passive. This is an extension of Harrigan's (1984, 1985a) work, which identifies operating ventures as those equity joint ventures that "carry out a productive economic activity" in which "[e]ach partner takes an active role in decision-making, if not also in the child's operations." The active decision-making role suggests that operating ventures are more interdependent than passive ventures (Contractor and Lorange, 1988). In the China context, both equity and contractual joint ventures meet the operating criteria identified above. Similarities in productive economic activity, decision-making structure, and tax treatment (Larson, 1988) suggest that, in Sino–foreign equity and contractual joint ventures, the distinction that operating ventures must form a separate entity diminishes in importance. We categorize the involvement mode in alliances meeting the first criteria outlined above as *operating*.

Passive ventures are defined as those where parties are not involved in the new entity's *strategic* business decisions (Harrigan, 1984, 1985a). Kim (1988) suggests that, with lower levels of uncertainty, alliance partners are inclined to use passive contracts, such as technology licensing, while partners hedge against higher levels of uncertainty by taking equity positions to ensure decision-making control over allocation decisions after uncertain outcomes are observed. Thus, operating ventures are hypothesized to be associated with higher levels of outcome uncertainty, and passive ventures are hypothesized to be associated with lower levels of outcome uncertainty. We identify the involvement mode of alliances in which *any* partner is not directly involved in ongoing operations and strategic decision making as *passive*.

Types of alliances

As shown in Figure 1, combination of the *reciprocal* and *contractual* obligation modes with the *operating* and *passive* involvement modes produces four alliance types: (1) Operating Reciprocal Alliances (ORAs)—commonly called equity joint ventures; (2) Operating Contractual Alliances (OCAs)—commonly called contractual joint ventures; (3) Passive Contractual Alliances (PCAs), which include oil-exploration consortia and research consortia; and (4) Passive Reciprocal Alliances (PRAs), which include counter-trade and counter-purchase agreements, process/assembly and buyback agreements, long-term licensing agreements, and dynamic technology-transfer agreements. Examples of all four types are presented in Figure 1.

Variations in operational characteristics

The different types of Sino–foreign business alliances are associated with variations in operational characteristics that have been identified as significant in the

```
            ALLIANCE-RELATED DECISION-MAKING CONTROL
               TASK & ORGANIZATIONAL COMPLEXITY
                 TASK & OUTCOME UNCERTAINTY
    HIGH          <-------PARTNER INTERDEPENDENCE-------->         LOW
  |----------------------------------------------------------------|
  |                                                                |
  |  ORAs             OCAs             PCAs             PRAs        |
  |  Operating        Operating        Passive          Passive     |
  |  Reciprocal       Contractual      Contractual      Reciprocal |
  |  Alliance         Alliance         Alliance         Alliance   |
  |                                                                |
  |----------------------------------------------------------------|
    LOW          <----PARENTAL OPERATING AUTONOMY---->        HIGH
                      & STRATEGIC FLEXIBILITY
```

Figure 2. Operational characteristic variations across alliance types

literature and in our research. Operational characteristic variations among the alliance types are observed in (1) operating autonomy (Killing, 1983; Tomlinson, 1970); (2) parental strategic flexibility (Harrigan 1985b; Killing, 1983); (3) partner interdependence (Contractor and Lorange, 1988; Killing, 1988); (4) alliance-related strategic and operating decision-making control (Killing, 1983; Harrigan, 1984, 1985b; Kim, 1988); (5) task uncertainty (Galbraith, 1973); (6) task and organizational complexity (Killing, 1988); and (7) outcome uncertainty associated with the alliance (Contractor and Lorange, 1988; Kim, 1988). Variations among the four alliance types relating to these operational characteristics can be illustrated on a continuum ranging from high to low, as represented in Figure 2. Although "high" and "low" are crude measures, they are sufficient to demonstrate the relative trade-offs among the alliance types.

Strategic flexibility is a function of parental operating autonomy. The higher the degree of operating autonomy, the higher the degree of strategic flexibility. Among alliances, PRAs provide the most parental operating autonomy and the most strategic flexibility, and ORAs the least. Nike, for example, had process-buyback agreements (PRAs) with several Chinese manufacturers. When Nike encountered quality and delivery problems from some of these suppliers, they were quickly able to retrench to two manufacturers who were able to meet Nike's specifications and delivery requirements. On the other hand, when the Beijing Jeep ORA was unable to generate sufficient foreign-exchange currency to purchase Jeep kits, this equity joint venture ground to a halt and required U.S. and Chinese governmental intervention before production resumed. Nike had more operating autonomy, and thus, more strategic flexibility to deal with the obstacles encountered than did AMC, Beijing Jeep's U.S. parent.

Parental operating autonomy and partner interdependence are reciprocal: the more interdependent the partners are, the less operating autonomy either parent enjoys. The more interdependent the partners, the more they engage in joint activity, a fact that inhibits unilateral action. In ORAs and OCAs, partners are highly interdependent and jointly carry out strategic and operating decision making relating to alliance activities, and engage in joint production or service delivery. However, in PCAs, only some partners engage in these activities, and in PRAs the degree of engagement approaches "arm's length." Partners in PCAs report higher levels of satisfaction with these alliances than do partners in ORAs and OCAs, despite the fact that these appear to be profitable more quickly than PCAs (Teagarden, 1990).

Alliance-related decision-making control is also a function of partner interdependence—the more interdependent the partners, the more they share operating decision-making control. However, while shared decision making represents a decrease in unilateral (individual partner) decision-making control, particularly strategic control, it does not suggest an absence of control (Killing, 1983; Schaan, 1983). Kim (1988) has found that, given the expectation of uncertain outcomes, TNCs opt for ORAs to maximize their control over those uncertain outcomes.

Identification of typological variations in operational characteristics and associated opportunities and constraints afford TNCs the opportunity to proactively enter and manage alliances. TNCs can identify the mode of engagement most consistent with their goals and objectives, given the opportunities and constraints associated with the various alliance types. Nike, for example, has consistently avoided the use of ORAs despite urging to do so from Chinese officials—to do so would not be consistent with their current strategy. Additionally, in the face of known operating constraints, TNCs can structure and staff alliances to attenuate anticipated negative outcomes. ORAs have built mechanisms into the contract to circumvent (or at least soften) constraints presented by loss of unilateral decision-making control, by, for example, including specific resolution procedures to address possible decision-making stalemates. In addition, some alliances are selecting expatriates for Sino–foreign alliance assignments, who are more tolerant of the constraints imposed by these interdependent operations.

Implications for research and practice

Sino–foreign strategic alliance discussion and research have been clouded by imprecision. For example, all four alliance types presented have been called "joint ventures." The Sino–foreign business alliance typology presented can serve as a common basis for systematic prescriptive research and theory building into this growing phenomenon. Use of the typology has enabled us to contrast variations in operational characteristics and discuss these, albeit to a limited degree, in light of our Sino–foreign alliance case-study data. The range of operational characteristics examined is far from exhaustive, and measures used to differentiate variation are crude. However, we are satisfied that we have demonstrated the utility of this systematic approach as a mechanism to inform research and practice.

For example, the regrettable events of the June 1989 Tiananmen incident resulted in a mass exodus of foreign expatriates from alliances in the PRC. Many negotiations in progress were put on hold and there was increased uncertainty regarding future business opportunities in the PRC (Ignatius and Bennett, 1989; Yang, 1989; Yankee Go Home, 1989). Less than six months later, many had returned to resume business activities, and it appears that those who returned most quickly were in ORAs or OCAs (Worthy, 1989). The U.S. firms that returned countered potential U.S. trade sanctions by claiming that their presence in the PRC furthered the cause of democracy or helped the Chinese people (Crouch, 1989; Smith, 1989; Worthy, 1989). This behavior on the part of ORAs and OCAs is predictable, based on the relatively low parental operating autonomy and low strategic flexibility associated with these types: they had to return to protect their investments. PRAs (and to a lesser degree PCAs) were able to withdraw from the PRC or to restructure existing contracts in the PRC because of greater operating autonomy and strategic flexibility. Many of these firms (and some ORAs and OCAs) used the Tiananmen incident as a justification for retrenching from alliances that were not meeting their expectations.

This study is best viewed as a starting point for future Sino–foreign strategic alliance research. Further development and refinement of the typology and related operating characteristic variations could prove fruitful for future empirical research as well as theory building. Questions such as the following could occupy an important role in future research: What are the strategic implications of the trade-offs among operational characteristics? How should firms select one operating mode over another? How should the influence of operational characteristics on alliance performance be evaluated? How should operational characteristics be measured? Which operational characteristics remain unidentified? Are the criteria upon which the typology is based the most appropriate? Is the typology exhaustive?

The wisdom consistently offered by those engaged in the management of Sino–foreign strategic business alliances is that the PRC is not for novices in international business. The successful management of Sino–foreign alliances is fraught with obstacles and constraints that challenge seasoned international veterans, and the challenges ahead are significant. However, systematic research of these alliances should enable us to understand and anticipate these challenges, and, through understanding and anticipation, to meet them.

Acknowledgments

Portions of earlier versions of this paper were presented at the Pan Pacific Conference V, Singapore, May 1988; Annual Academy of Management Meeting, Anaheim, CA, August 1987; and the International Symposium on Pacific Asian

Business, Honolulu, HI, January 1989. They are included in the Pan Pacific Conference V Proceedings and the International Symposium on Pacific Asian Business Proceedings.

The authors wish to thank Paul Beamish, Richard Wright, John Frankenstein, Oded Shenkar, and others for their insightful comments on earlier versions of this paper.

References

Beamish, P. W. (1985) "The Characteristics of Joint Ventures in Developed and Developing Countries." *Columbia Journal of World Business*, Fall, pp. 13–19.

Beamish, P. W., and Banks, J. C. (1987) "Equity Joint Ventures and the Theory of the Multinational Enterprise." *Journal of International Business Studies*, Summer, pp. 1–16.

Campbell, N. (1985) *China Strategies*. Manchester: University of Manchester Press.

Contractor, F. J., and Lorange, P. (1988) "Why Should Firms Cooperate? The Strategy and Economics for Cooperative Ventures." In F. J. Contractor and P. Lorange, eds., *Cooperative Strategy in International Business*, pp. 3–30. Lexington, MA: Lexington Books.

Crouch, G. (1989) "Political Crisis Poses Ethical Challenge for US Firms in China." *Los Angeles Times*, Friday, June 23, D1.

"Foreign Devils Pack Their Bags." (1989) *The Economist*, June 10, p. 22.

Galbraith, J. (1973) *Designing Complex Organizations*. Menlo Park, NJ: Addison-Wesley.

Harrigan, K. R. (1984) "Joint Ventures and Global Strategies." *Columbia Journal of World Business*, 19 (2), pp. 7–17.

_____. (1985a) *Strategies for Joint Ventures*. Lexington, MA: Lexington Books.

_____. (1985b) *Strategic Flexibility: A Management Guide for Changing Times*. Lexington, MA: Lexington Books.

Ignatius, A., and Bennett, A. (1989) "Beijing's Economic Ills Pose a New Threat of Social Upheaval. *Wall Street Journal*, Thursday, August 4, A1 and A12.

Johnston, W. J. (1989) "No Turning Back for China." *Los Angeles Times*, June 18, IV3.

Killing, J. P. (1983) *Strategies for Joint Venture Success*. New York: Praeger.

_____. (1988) "Understanding Alliances: The Role of Task and Organizational Complexity." In F. J. Contractor and P. Lorange, eds., *Cooperative Strategies in International Business*, pp. 55–68. Lexington, MA: Lexington Books.

Kim, Y. K. (1988) Strategic Competition in Negotiations of International Technology Licensing: The Informational Interaction View. Unpublished doctoral dissertation, University of California, Los Angeles, Los Angeles, CA.

Larson, M. R. (1988) "Exporting Private Enterprise to Developing Communist Countries: A Case Study on China." *Columbia Journal of World Business*, 23 (1), pp. 79–87.

National Council for U.S.–China Trade. (1987) *U.S. Joint Ventures in China: A Progress Report*. Washington, D.C.: Department of Commerce.

Schaan, J. L. (1983) Parent Control and Joint Venture Success: The Case of Mexico. Unpublished doctoral dissertation. Ontario, Canada: University of Western Ontario.

Schnepp, O. A.; Von Glinow, M. A.; and Bhambri, A. (1990) *U.S.–China Technology Transfer*. Englewood Cliffs, NJ: Prentice Hall,.

Smith, A. (1989) "China: Will the Open Door Close?" *Adam Smith's Money World*, Air date June 9. Educational Broadcasting Corporation, Transcript #533, pp.1–4.

Teagarden, M. B. (1990) Sino–U.S. Joint Venture Effectiveness. Unpublished doctoral dissertation, University of Southern California, Los Angeles, CA.

Teagarden, M. B., and Von Glinow, M. A. (1988) "Sino–U.S. Business Alliances: Toward Typological Clarification." *Proceedings of the Pan-Pacific Conference V*, Singapore, pp. 319–323.

_____. (1990) "When Is a Joint Venture a Joint Venture? The Classification of Sino–Foreign Strategic Business Alliances." *International Symposium on Pacific Asian Business Proceedings*, Honolulu, HI, pp. 56–59.

Tomlinson, J. W. C. (1970) *The Joint Venture Process in International Business: India and Pakistan*. Cambridge, MA: MIT Press.

Von Glinow, M. A.; Schnepp, O.; and Bhambri, A. (1988) "Assessing Success in U.S.–China Technology Transfer." In T. Agmon and M. A. Von Glinow, eds., *The Dialectics of Technology Transfer*. Oxford University Press, forthcoming.

Von Glinow, M. A., and Teagarden, M. B. (1988) "The Transfer of Human Resource Management Technology in Sino–U.S. Cooperative Ventures: Problems and Solutions." *Human Resource Management*, Summer, 27 (2).

_____. (1989) "Contextually Embedded Influences on Cooperative Alliance Performance: The Case of Sino–U.S. Joint Ventures." *Proceedings of the Pan Pacific Conference VI*, Sydney, Australia, pp. 259–260.

Wang, N. T. (1984) *China's Modernization and Transnational Corporations*. Lexington, MA: Lexington Books.

Worthy, F. S. (1989) "Doing Business in China Now." *Fortune*, Pacific Rim 1989, Fall, pp. 21–32.

Wright, R. W. (1981) "Evolving International Business Arrangements." In K. C. Dhawan, H. Etemad, and R. W. Wright, eds., *International Business: A Canadian Perspective*. Don Mills, Ontario: Addison-Wesley.

Yang, D.; Javetski, B.; and Holstein, W. J. (1989) "The Outside World Puts China on Hold. *Business Week*, July 10, pp. 40–41.

"Yankee Gone Home" (1989) *The Economist*, June 24, p. 66.

Yue Haltao (1987) "Three Forms of Investment Called for." *Beijing Review*, June 1, pp. 21–22.

MEE-KAU NYAW

The Significance and Managerial Roles of Trade Unions in Joint Ventures with China

Introduction

Since the People's Republic of China (PRC) opened up its economy to foreign investment in 1979, it has attracted U.S.$2.82 billion direct foreign investment into the country during 1979–88 (*Statistical Yearbook of China*, various years). Broadly speaking, there are four types of direct foreign investment in China: equity joint ventures, cooperative ventures (or "contractual joint ventures"), wholly foreign-owned enterprises, and cooperative development (offshore oil drilling) ventures. Equity joint ventures accounted for 31.5 percent of the country's total direct foreign investment during the period 1979–88 and were favored by U.S., Japanese, and European investors (*Statistical Yearbook of China*, various years, and National Council for U.S.–China Trade, 1987).

The success of a joint venture enterprise in China depends not only on favorable macro-environmental variables such as political, economic, and sociocultural factors, but also on its management. Most studies on management issues to date focused on the management system, organizational structure, size and efficiency, employee relations, and culture (Zamet and Bovarnick, 1986; Davidson, 1987; Henley and Nyaw, 1989; Nyaw and Lin, 1988; Shenkar, 1988). This paper analyzes one missing link that has not been explored, namely, the significance and managerial roles of trade unions in joint ventures in China, since they are significantly different from their counterparts in the state-owned enterprises.

This paper will first examine some general features of trade unions in the joint ventures vis-à-vis state-owned enterprises. It then looks at the structural attributes and roles of the trade unions by focusing on their interlocking relationships with the enterprise, the state, the Chinese Communist Party (CCP), and the mass organizations such as the Communist Youth League and Women's Federation.

The author is Chairman of the Department of Organization and Management at The Chinese University of Hong Kong, Shatin, Hong Kong.

The paper also illustrates and discusses the empirical results of the relative importance of the various roles of trade unions, as perceived by the union cadres in the joint ventures of Shenzhen Special Economic Zone (SEZ). It concludes with a discussion of the roles of trade unions and the future prospects of joint ventures' employee relations in China.

Some salient features of the trade unions of joint ventures vis-à-vis state-owned enterprises

The communist ideology dictates that workers are "masters of the house." Therefore, workers' participation in management takes place in most communist countries, although it varies in form. The workers' participation in Chinese state-owned enterprises is carried out through the workers' congress, which is an agency of power in the enterprise. Among other things, it has the power to (1) examine and adopt resolutions submitted by factory directors on production plans, budgets, etc.; (2) discuss and decide on the use of funds, regulations for awarding or penalizing workers and staff; (3) approve reforms on management structure and wage adjustments; (4) recommend leading cadres for commendation or promotion; and (5) elect administrators, subject to approval and appointment by the appropriate higher authorities (Henley and Nyaw, 1986, pp. 646–647).

The enterprise trade-union committee is another important pillar in the decision-making structure of state-owned enterprises in China. The trade union is considered a school of Communism and a "transmission belt" linking the party with the masses (Lenin's doctrine). It is also regarded as a school of management for workers. In China, an enterprise trade-union committee acts as an agent to help implement the decisions made by the workers' congress. Its other functions, authorities, and responsibilities include (1) to protect workers' rights and material interests; (2) to cooperate with enterprise managers in carrying out state decrees concerning workers' interest and welfare; (3) to organize workers in running the enterprise; (4) to prepare for the convocation of workers' congress, elect delegates, deal with workers' appeals, etc.; and (5) to serve as an executive body when the workers' congress is not in session, overseeing the implementation of congress resolutions (Henley and Nyaw, 1986; Nelson and Reeder, 1985; Littler and Lockett, 1983).

Joint ventures are new in China. According to the 1979 Law on Chinese–Foreign Joint Ventures (hereafter Joint Venture Law), there is no upper limit to foreign investment in a joint venture, but the law sets a minimum of 25 percent for investment by foreign party or parties (Article 4, Joint Venture Law, 1979). Ideologically, the establishment of joint ventures in China poses the following dilemmas for the CCP. First, is the profit-making international joint venture compatible with the ideals of communism and socialism? The views expounded by Xu Dixin, a noted Chinese economist, seemed to be shared by most high-ranking Chinese communist leaders. According to Xu, Chinese joint ventures, cooperative ventures, and compensation trade are all "state capitalist enterprises," and "state capitalism" may exist in a socialist nation. However, activities and operations of a joint venture are subject to the regulation of the state (Xu, 1982). As China is now considered to be in the "primary stage of socialism," as argued by the Chinese communist leadership, the coexistence of joint ventures and state-owned enterprises is allowed. Furthermore, joint ventures in China are under the control of state regulations that protect worker interests.

Second, in contrast to state-owned enterprises, workers and staff of joint ventures are no longer the "masters of the house." One unionist in Shenzhen even suggested that "there is exploitation because of state capitalism" (*South China Morning Post*, November 13, 1988). However, there is an opposite view that the exploitation of workers by foreign investors is incorrect. Tang argued that employee relations in joint ventures in the PRC are different from those of the capitalist countries (Tang, 1988, p. 244). No conclusion has been arrived at regarding this theoretical issue to date. We will set aside this issue and concentrate on the discussion of how the labor management system works in China.

As stipulated in the Constitution of the Trade Unions of the PRC, trade union organizations in joint ventures are an integral part of the All-China Federation of Trade Unions (ACFTU), but "provisions dealing with the special problems of trade unions in such enterprises are stipulated separately by the ACFTU" (Article 35, Constitution of the Trade Unions of the PRC, 1983). Unfortunately, ACFTU to date has no provision dealing with trade unions specifically. Instead, provisions dealing with the joint ventures in China are contained in two separate sources. In the "Provisions for Trade Unions of Special Economic Zone Enterprises in Guangdong Province," it is stipulated that trade unions in such enterprises (including joint ventures) are legal entities and the chairmen of trade unions are their representatives (Article 3). On the other hand, the Joint Venture Law stipulates that a joint venture is a limited-liability company (Article 4, Joint Venture Law). Trade unions are therefore not appendages of the joint venture. Trade unions have been formed in most joint ventures in the PRC in accordance with the Joint Venture Law. However, they are not mandatory. Ninty-two percent of foreign or foreign participating firms have their trade unions set up in Shenzhen in 1987 (*Shenzhen SEZ Daily*, April 16, 1987). Although there is no workers' congress in a joint venture, the "Regulations for the Implementation of the Law of the PRC on Chinese–Foreign Joint Ventures, 1983" (hereafter Joint Venture Implementation Regulations, 1983) stipulates that there is a need for the enterprise "to heed the opinions" of staff and workers, particularly on labor-related issues. However, the extent of worker participation in management is far less than in state-owned enterprises. This issue will be elaborated in the following section in connection with the interlocking relationships between trade unions and the boards of directors of joint ventures.

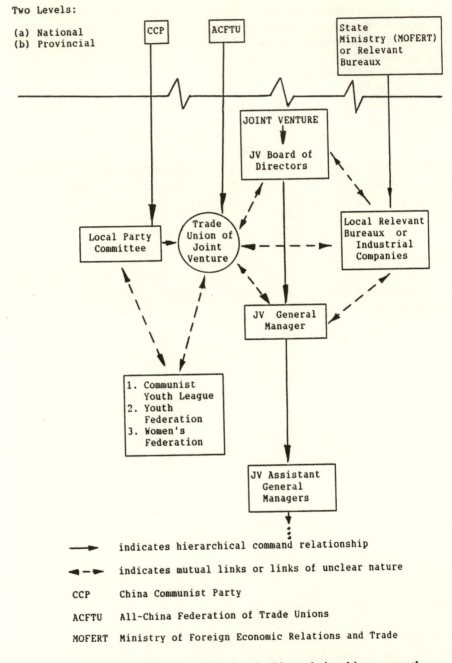

Two Levels:

(a) National
(b) Provincial

CCP

ACFTU

State Ministry (MOFERT) or Relevant Bureaux

JOINT VENTURE

JV Board of Directors

Local Party Committee

Trade Union of Joint Venture

Local Relevant Bureaux or Industrial Companies

JV General Manager

1. Communist Youth League
2. Youth Federation
3. Women's Federation

JV Assistant General Managers

⟶   indicates hierarchical command relationship

◄ ─ ►   indicates mutual links or links of unclear nature

CCP   China Communist Party

ACFTU   All-China Federation of Trade Unions

MOFERT   Ministry of Foreign Economic Relations and Trade

Figure 1. A simplified diagram of the interlocking relationships among the trade union, joint venture management, state ministry, and the party

Structural attributes and managerial roles
of trade unions in the joint venture

The significance and structural attributes of the trade unions in the Chinese joint ventures is shown in Figure 1. We shall first briefly look at the organization and management system of a joint venture and its interlocking relationships with the trade union committee.

The Joint Venture Law stipulates that the joint venture's board of directors, which consists of no fewer than three members, shall be the highest organ of authority. It decides all major issues relating to the enterprise such as

> expansion programs, proposal for production and operation activities, the budget for revenues and expenditures, distribution of profits, plans concerning manpower and scales, the termination of business and the appointment or employment of the president, the vice-presidents (or general manager, and deputy manager[s]), the chief engineer, the treasurer and auditors, as well as their powers and terms of employment, etc." (Article 6, Joint Venture Law 1979)

Decision through consultation of the respective parties concerned is emphasized in handling major issues or problems. It is also stipulated that the chairman of the board shall be appointed by the Chinese side, and its vice chairman by the foreign investor (Articles 33–34, Chapter V, Joint Venture Implementation Regulations, 1983). The responsibilities of day-to-day operations and management rest with the general managers, who "within the scope authorized by the board of directors, represent the joint venture in external matters and, within the venture, appoint and dismiss subordinate personnel, and exercise the other powers conferred upon them by the board of directors" (Article 39, Implementation Regulations).

Unlike its counterpart in the West, the "management" of a joint venture is supposed to "positively support" the work and activities of its trade union (Chen and Li, 1987, p. 87). Union representatives have the right to sit in on the board of directors' meeting to air workers' opinions, although they do not have the right to vote.

Although a joint venture has autonomy over its operations and management, it is under the jurisdiction of the Ministry of Foreign Economic Relations and Trade (MOFERT) or its authorized agents. The Foreign Investment Commission of MOFERT approves a joint venture's application for establishment under the Joint Venture Implementation Regulations. After a venture is established, MOFERT (or its authorized agents) is responsible for guiding, assisting, or supervising the implementation of the joint venture contract, but is prohibited from issuing directives to the venture. For example, a joint venture is assisted by government authorities who guarantee the venture's priority access to resources, but will leave the joint venture to work out its own production and operating plans. In the past, government departments dealt mainly with the general managers of the joint ventures. During interviews in Shenzhen by this author in 1988, it was discovered that government agencies have a tendency to deal more with the board of directors. As there are no specific rules or guidelines to follow, this poses some problems to the operation of joint ventures.

China considers it the political right of staff and workers to join a trade union in the joint venture. The trade union of a joint venture, like its counterpart in any enterprise in China, is a member of the local union for a particular industry or the local trade union council. Theoretically, the general objectives of the joint ventures are in line with those of the trade unions, i.e., to make the venture a success. A successful joint venture benefits both the foreign investors (in the form of "profit") and the nation (in the form of technology transfer and foreign-exchange earnings). However, it is emphasized that the trade union of a joint venture has a duty to represent the interests of the staff and workers, and "shall have the right to represent them in signing labor contracts with the joint venture and supervising the implementation of such contracts" (Article 96, Joint Venture Implementation Regulations).

Staff and workers in the state-owned enterprises are known to have enjoyed the "iron rice bowl," a form of lifetime job tenure. Beginning in October 1986, workers in these enterprises are employed on contracted terms on an experimental basis, as part of the country's labor management reforms (*Ming Pao*, July 29, 1986 and *Wen Wei Pao*, September 5, 1986). According to the new regulations, workers can theoretically be dismissed. However, it is widely known that workers in state-owned enterprises are dismissed only in exceptional cases, such as political purges or serious offenses. The "lifetime job tenure system" still exists, though not necessarily in name. In contrast, the "iron rice bowl" is not applicable to staff and workers in joint ventures in China. A joint venture has the right to lay off staff and workers whose employment is considered redundant (Provisions of the PRC for Labor Management in Chinese–Foreign Joint Venture, 1986). It can also fire undisciplined workers or those who have committed serious offenses. This has in fact taken place. China Hewlett-Packard Ltd. fired nine workers (*Hong Kong Economic Journal*, June 28, 1987), and a successful Hong Kong–Chinese joint venture manufacturer of matchbox toys in Shanghai has dismissed eleven workers since its establishment in 1986 (Koo, 1987). None encountered opposition from the trade unions. On the contrary, they had the latter's support, since the reasons for the dismissals were justified.

State-owned enterprises have little control over the employment of workers and staff. They have to take whoever is assigned to them by the state labor bureau. Workers and staff literally have no mobility once they are attached to a "unit." Although labor management reform has been introduced in the last few years, it is carried out only on a limited scale. The reform so far has achieved little success, as enterprises are very reluctant to release their own workers. Without the permission of existing enterprises, other "units" could not take them. In contrast, the workers and staff of joint ventures are hired by the enterprise through the labor service company with approval from the labor bureau. A joint venture may also advertise for workers. Successful candidates may undergo a three-to-six-month probation period, a practice commonly found in a market economy.

One unique aspect of the trade unions of joint ventures in China is that they deal directly with foreign partners or their representatives with regard to labor disputes or grievance. They are not dealing with the joint ventures *per se,* as the latter are owned partly by the state. Unions are a transmission belt between the party and the masses. They are not supposed to "negotiate" with the party-controlled state. In dealing with foreign investors, union representatives need considerable skills in negotiation, which they tend to lack. The Chinese emphasize "consultation" rather than "confrontation" in dealing with most matters. Should a labor dispute such as a worker's dismissal not be resolved through consultation, one or both parties can request arbitration from the local government, in accordance with the Provision for Labor Management in Chinese–Foreign Joint Ventures (Article 4). However, arbitration seems to be rare in Chinese joint ventures. In contrast to the adversarial roles of many trade unions in Western countries, the Chinese partners emphasize that the trade unions of joint ventures in China are cooperative and conciliatory. Among other things, they organize vocational, scientific, and technical studies, and they educate the workers to observe labor discipline and to fulfill the economic task of the enterprise. Joint ventures have to allot a sum equal to 2 percent of the actual wages of all staff and workers as union funds to finance these activities (Articles 98–99, Implementation Regulations). As a high-ranking official from MOFERT remarked, the role of trade unions of joint ventures in China is different:

> A foreign investor need not worry about the union being unproductive toward the management or the Chinese employees being insubordinate to the foreign managers. Experience proves that, with the guidance of their trade unions, the Chinese staff and workers are highly conscientious, disciplined and industrious employees working for the interest of the ventures. (Chu, 1986, p. 80)

Although the above remarks are promotional in tone, they nonetheless portray the task of trade unions of the ventures as perceived by the Chinese authority. The trade unions certainly have no intention of disrupting the operations of joint ventures, as the Chinese Communist Party has repeatedly educated workers that it would be in the mutual interests of the state and foreign partners if staff and workers work diligently and efficiently for the joint ventures that employ them (Tang, 1988, pp. 244–249).

The management of Chinese state-owned enterprises involve the intricacies of four actors: the enterprise's party secretary, the factory director, the workers' congress, and the enterprise trade union (Henley and Nyaw, 1986). In the joint venture enterprise, the law does not stipulate the role or formation of a communist party committee. In one episode cited, the board of directors rejected a request for help to set up a party organization in a joint venture, and no objection was raised by the Chinese side (Horsley, 1984, p. 21). On the other hand, the Chinese leadership seems to favor some form of party organization to be established in the international joint ventures but does not insist on it (Tang, 1988, p. 251). Irrespective of the existence of party organization, the author's interviews in the Shenzhen Special Economic Zone (SEZ) in 1988 revealed that party activities do exist and are normally carried out by the trade unions. The influence of the CCP is also felt through the state-appointed directors. One of the intricacies of the whole system is that most senior trade unionists and directors are party members themselves, and they strictly adhere to the party line and policy. The party's activities in the joint ventures are mainly to indoctrinate staff and workers to adhere to the party line and to work in harmony with the investors (Tang, 1988, p. 251).

Apart from trade unions, other mass organizations such as the Communist Youth League, Youth Federation, and Women's Federation also exist in the joint ventures just like in many "units," including state-owned enterprises in China. Their activities are channeled through the trade unions of joint ventures (see Figure 1). The author's interviews revealed that the secretary of the local Communist Youth League is usually the vice president of the joint venture's trade union or a member of its executive committee. As compared to trade unions, the roles played by other mass organizations are far less significant. They organize mainly social support functions.

Some empirical results of the relative importance of various roles of trade unions

The foregoing section illustrates some of the principal roles played by trade unions of joint ventures. A survey was undertaken to find out the actual roles as perceived by union cadres in the Shenzhen SEZ in late 1988. In this survey, the trade union's roles were first divided into twenty-three items, which were then reclassified into eight separate main groups. These roles are mainly stipulated in the "Provisions of Trade Unions of Shenzhen SEZ in Guangdong Province, 1985" and in the Joint Venture Law and Implementation Regulations. The eight main groups of roles in trade unions are as follows (items under each main groups are illustrated in the Appendix):

1. To participate in the important decision making of operations and management of the joint venture;
2. To participate in the formulation of the venture's regulations and rules in relating to staff and workers;

3. To represent and reflect the interests of staff and workers;

4. To enhance and improve the quality of staff and workers;

5. To monitor and assist the staff and workers in fulfilling the economic tasks of the enterprise;

6. To monitor the execution of government laws and regulations by the enterprise;

7. To monitor management personnel of the joint venture; and

8. To promote social relationships.

The questionnaire was phrased in Chinese. Eighteen high-ranking union cadres from different joint ventures in Shenzhen SEZ were asked to rate the roles from item (1) to item (23), as shown in the Appendix, on the following six-point scale during interviews conducted in Chinese: extremely important (6 points), very important (5 points), important (4 points), moderately important (3 points), less important (2 points), and unimportant (1 point). The median score for each role item was then taken as its central-tendency value.

All the joint ventures under survey were established in the last few years. The history of the trade unions in joint ventures in China is also short, and their levels of development are uneven. Generally speaking, the trade unions of the joint ventures under survey have been fairly well developed.

The results of the average score for each item as perceived by the union cadres are presented in Table 1. Table 2 gives the relative importance of the union's roles classified by groups, and their respective rankings based on the average scores of role items under each group.

The empirical results indicate the following important aspects. First, the trade union's role as a representative of the interests of staff and workers and as a provider of services for them are most significant and important. For example, issues regarding dismissals, grievances, and the provisions for cultural, recreational, and sports activities were rated very high. Second, the role of workers' participation in the management of the joint ventures' operations and development activities (such as finance, strategic plans, and the formulation of the rules and regulations) was very insignificant. Third, the role of monitoring staff and workers in fulfilling the economic tasks of the enterprises as well as in monitoring management personnel was of moderate importance.

The foregoing empirical results regarding the roles of trade unions as perceived by senior union cadres of joint ventures in Shenzhen demonstrate the current thinking of the Chinese Communist Party in view of the fact that trade unionists cannot deviate from the party line. The party is more concerned with the well-being of workers of joint ventures. Despite trade unions being vested with the power to participate in the enterprise's management, such participation is considered less important by union cadres. This finding is consistent with the report of two foreign investigators in their interview with a Chinese official: the labor union of a Chinese joint venture is not the labor union they understand in

**Table 1.   Relative importance of the role items as perceived
by union cadres (median scores) *n* = 18**

degree of importance	*role items*
extremely important	to be consulted on dismissal and penalty of staff and workers
very important	to organize cultural, recreational and sports activities
	to do ideological and political work for staff and workers so as to effectively carry out production and to abide by laws and regulations
	to monitor the execution of environmental and safety regulations
	to monitor the execution of labor insurance regulations
	to monitor the execution of production safety regulations
important	to represent staff and workers in signing labor contracts
	to use union funds rationally for the benefit of staff and workers
	to resolve conflicts between workers and enterprises
	to conduct technological-development and management training courses
	to assist staff and workers to observe the various regulations of the joint ventures
	to promote friendship and understanding between local workers and expatriate staffs
moderately important	to ensure staff and workers to carry out work as prescribed in the labor contract
	to encourage staff and workers to carry out technological-innovation and labor-emulation campaigns
	to monitor the promotion and appointment of management staff
	to monitor the violation and offence of laws by management staff
less important	to discuss important issues concerning production and operation activities
	to study salary and wage regulations for staff and workers
	to study the reward and penalty system for staff and workers
	to study the welfare regulations for staff and workers
	to study the labor insurance regulations for staff and workers
unimportant	to discuss the expansion and development plans of the joint venture
	to monitor the enterprise's abidance by the finance and tax laws of the country

**Table 2. Relative importance of the roles of trade unions
(classified by groups) as perceived by union cadres**
(Maximum score = 6) n = 18

roles classified by groups	average scores	rankings of importance
I. To participate in the important decision making of operations and management of the joint venture	1.5	6
II. To participate in the formulation of the venture's regulations and rules in relating to staff and workers	2.0	5
III. To represent and reflect the interests of staff and workers	4.5	2
IV. To enhance and improve the quality of staff and workers	5.0	1
V. To monitor and assist the staff and workers in fulfilling the economic tasks of the enterprise	3.4	4
VI. To monitor the execution of governmental laws and regulations by the enterprise	4.0	3
VII. To monitor the management personnel of the venture	3.0	4
VIII. To promote social relationships	4.0	3

Note: Sub-items under each groups are given in the Appendix.

the West, "it is a management-assistance tool and it is also an organization that looks after the personal needs and the welfare of the employees" (Zamet and Bovarnick, 1986, p. 17).

Although the trade unions of the joint ventures do not play an adversarial role, the power is not all one-sided in favor of management. Joint ventures are highly dependent on the trade union to elicit extra effort from the workforce, particularly during the peak production period (Koo, 1987). In certain cases, management needs to pay attention to the resistance of workers. For example, a joint venture (in Sichuan) to make television sets, using a Japanese continuous assembly line technology, had to be abandoned because female workers simply refused to accept the discipline required. Instead, a slower paced and multi-operation assembly system was adopted rather than the original, more highly differentiated and deskilled Japanese system (Henley and Nyaw, 1986, p. 648).

Conclusion

The trade union of a joint venture in the PRC plays an important role in the political education of the workforce, inculcating the workers with the virtues of diligence and hard work. In contrast to state-owned enterprises, a party committee is generally non-existent or is not a formal organization in international joint ventures, if it exists. The trade union is therefore charged with the above responsibilities, which are generally the task of the party committee. However, senior union cadres in the joint ventures are also party members, with few exceptions. They may wear different hats so that the distinction of their identities is ambiguous.

At present, not all joint ventures have trade unions, particularly the smaller ones. Even if unions do exist, they may lack legal status in undertaking certain specific activities. For example, although it is stipulated in the Joint-Venture Law and its implementation regulations that trade unions have the right to attend meetings of the board of directors to discuss wide-ranging issues, including management operations and development plans, it was found during an investigation by this author in Shenzhen in 1988 that such a stipulation is not contained in some of the ventures' articles of association. This reduces the union's participation in management to a mere formalism. Those joint ventures with this stipulation embodied in the agreement may deliberately leave it to a broad interpretation or opt not to exercise it, except for labor-related issues. Even if they wish to use it, they usually lack the expertise required for the job. Managers and directors of the board are therefore the genuine "masters of the house" rather than the workers. This indicates the pragmatism of CCP and its willingness to abandon its ideological purity under certain circumstances.

The present industrial relations system of China's joint ventures seems to function well. Although bureaucrary and the indiscriminatory levy of fees not specified in the joint venture contracts are the subjects of common criticism by foreign investors, little has been reported on any malfunctioning of the trade unions. In addition, labor productivity in joint ventures in China is generally far higher than that of state-owned enterprises. This is due to better management of labor in joint ventures. Workers are more disciplined and financially motivated (Henley and Nyaw, 1989; Pi et al., 1989). Undoubtedly, joint venture has the support of trade unionists. One prominent Hong Kong entrepreneur, who has successfully invested in a joint venture in Shanghai, noted: "I urge Hong Kong entrepreneurs not to the oppose establishment of trade unions (as in Hong Kong); the union has assisted the workers greatly in fulling the economic tasks of my enterprise" (Koo, 1987).

The analyses of the significance and roles of trade unions demonstrate that the Chinese are not inclined to take drastic measures that may jeopardize the confidence of foreign investors. This is true even after the recent Tiananmen massacre. China has officially announced that its open-door policy will remain unchanged. It has made strenuous efforts to woo Hong Kong and Western capitalists to invest in China after the June 4, 1989 incident in Beijing. Chinese trade unions could be expected to play a conciliatory role as in the past. It is unlikely that trade unions will become more militant as long as they are under the firm control of the Communist Party, and there is no clear sign to indicate that such control is fading.

Postscript

The PRC government had made a crucial amendment to the Joint Venture Law with regard to the organizational structure of a joint venture in China on April 4, 1990. As contrasted with the past, chairmanship of the board of directors will not be appointed by the Chinese side. Rather, it is subject to negotiation by both the Chinese partner and the foreign investor, or by election at the board meeting. Should the chairmanship go to a person from one side, the deputy chairmanship will then be a person from the other partner. This change could be interpreted as a major concession from the PRC. The relaxation of the stipulation on chairmanship of the board of directors is in line with the generally accepted practice of international joint ventures in most countries. Other than the above revision, as of June 1990 managerial roles in joint ventures as discussed in this article remain unchanged.

Acknowledgments

The author wishes to acknowledge the assistance of Mr. Lin Gong-Shi, School of Economics and Management, Tsinghua University, Beijing, for conducting the field survey. Views expressed in this paper, however, are solely the responsibility of the author.

References

Chen, S. F., and Li, P. K. (eds.) (1987) *The Management of Chinese–Foreign Joint Venture*. Shanghai: Kexue Puji Publisher (in Chinese).

"China's Unions Feeling a Chill." *South China Morning Post*, November 13, 1988.

Chu, Baotai (1986) *Foreign Investment in China: Questions and Answers*, Beijing: Foreign Languages Press.

Constitution of The Trade Unions of the People's Republic of China, adopted by 10th National Congress of Chinese Trade Unions on October 23, 1983.

Daniels, J. D.; Krug, J.; and Nigh, D. (1986) "U.S. Joint Ventures in China: Motivation and Management of Political Risks." *California Management Review*, 27(4), Summer, pp. 46–58.

Davidson, W. H. (1987) "Creating and Managing Joint Ventures in China." *California Management Review*, 29 (4), Summer, pp. 77–94.

Henley, J. S., and Nyaw, M. K. (1986) "Introducing Market Forces into Managerial Decision Making in Chinese Industrial Enterprises." *Journal of Management Studies*, 23 (6), pp. 635–656.

———. (1989) "The System of Management and Performance of Joint Ventures in China: Some Evidence From Shenzhen Special Economic Zone." In *Advances in Chinese Industrial Studies*, Vol.2, JAI Press (forthcoming).

Horsley, J. P. (1984) "Chinese Labor: Foreign Firms Are Learning How Hard It Is to Negotiate Realistic Labor Contracts in China." *China Business Review*, May/June, pp. 16–25.

"Joint Venture Enterprises Have Full Autonomy." *Hong Kong Economic Journal*, June 28, 1987.

Koo, S. K. (1987) "Understanding Business Relationship Between China and Hong Kong." *Speech* presented to a seminar organized by the Chinese Executives Club, Hong Kong Management Association, December 12, 1987.

Law of the People's Republic of China on Chinese–Foreign Joint Ventures, July 8, 1979.

Littler, C. R., and Lockett, M. (1983) "The Significance of Trade Unions in China." *Industrial Relations Journal*, 14 (4), Winter, pp. 31–42.

"Moody's Set to Review China Risk." *South China Morning Post*, June 10, 1989.

National Council for U.S.–China Trade (1987) *US Joint Ventures in China: A Progress Report*, Washington, D.C.

Nelson, J. A., and Reeder, J. A. (1985) "Labor Relations in China." *California Management Review*, 27 (4), Summer, pp. 13–32.

Nyaw, M. K., and Lin, G. S. (1988) "Organizational Size, Adjustment and Managerial Effectiveness of Joint Ventures in Shenzhen Special Economic Zone." In *Perspectives on China's Modernization: Studies on China's Open Policy and Special Economic Zones*, K. Y. Wong, C. C. Lau, and Eva B. C. Li, eds. Hong Kong: Centre for Contemporary Asian Studies, The Chinese University of Hong Kong, pp. 211–223.

Pi, J. S.; Chang, J.; et al. (1989) "Management of Foreign Enterprises: Problems and Thinking." *Jingji Lilun and Jingji Kuanli* 3, 63–68 (in Chinese).

"Positive Aspects of Union Organizations in Foreign Enterprises." *Shenzhen SEZ Daily*, April 16, 1987.

Provisions for Trade Unions of Special Economic Zone Enterprises in Guangdong Province, adopted on May 8, 1985.

Provisions of PRC for Labor Management in Chinese–Foreign Joint Ventures, July 26, 1986.

Regulations for the Implementation of the Law of the PRC on Chinese–Foreign Joint Venture, September 20, 1983.

Shenkar, O. (1988) "International Joint Ventures' Problems in China: Culture, Politics, or Organizational Structure?" Paper presented for the APROS Conference on *Firms, Management, the State and Economic Culture*, Hong Kong: April 6–9, 1988.

Statistical Yearbook of China. (various years) Beijing: China Statistical Bureau.

Tang, F. C. (1988) *Practice and Enquiry of Shenzhen's Utilization of Foreign Investment*, Shenzhen, China: Hai Tien Publisher (in Chinese).

Xu, Dixin (1982) "To Build Up Special Economic Zones Progressively and Steadily." In *An Enquiry into the Problems of Special Economic Zones*, Fujian People's Publication, pp. 1–10 (in Chinese).

Zamet, J. M., and Bovarnick, M. E. (1986) "Employee Relations for Multinational Companies in China." *Columbia Journal of World Business*, 21 (1), Spring, pp. 13–19.

Appendix: Roles of trade unions in joint ventures in China

I. To participate in the important decision making of operations and management of the joint venture:
   - (1) to discuss the expansion and development plans of the venture
   - (2) to discuss important issues concerning production and operation activities

II. To participate in the formulation of the venture's regulations and rules in relating to staff and workers:
   - (3) to study salary and wage regulations
   - (4) to study the reward and penalty system
   - (5) to study the welfare regulations
   - (6) to study the labor insurance regulations

III. To represent and reflect the interests of staff and workers:
   - (7) to represent staff and workers in signing labor contracts
   - (8) to be consulted on dismissal and penalty of staff and workers
   - (9) to use union funds rationally for the benefit of staff and workers
   - (10) to resolve conflicts between workers and enterprises

IV. To enhance and improve the quality of staff and workers:
   - (11) to do ideological and political work so as to effectively carry out production and to abide by laws and regulations
   - (12) to conduct technological development and management training courses
   - (13) to organize cultural, recreational, and sports activities

V. To monitor and assist the staff and workers in fulfilling the economic tasks of the enterprise:
   - (14) to ensure staff and workers carry out work as prescribed in the contract
   - (15) to assist staff and workers to observe the various regulations applying to the joint venture
   - (16) to encourage staff and workers to carry out technological innovation and labor-emulation campaigns

VI. To monitor the execution of governmental laws and regulations by the enterprise:
   - (17) execution of environmental and safety regulations
   - (18) execution of labor insurance regulations
   - (19) execution of production safety regulations
   - (20) to monitor the enterprise's abidance by finance and tax laws

VII. To monitor management personnel of the joint venture:
   - (21) promotion and appointment of management staff
   - (22) violation of laws by management

VIII. To promote social relationship:
   - (23) To promote friendship and understanding between local workers and expatriate staff.

Sources: Compiled from "Provisions of Trade Unions of Shenzhen Special Economic Zone in Guangdong Province, 1985," "Law of Chinese–Foreign Joint Ventures, 1979" and "Regulations for the Implementation of Chinese–Foreign Joint Venture Law, 1983."

INGA S. BAIRD, MARJORIE A. LYLES, SHAOBO JI, AND
ROBERT WHARTON

Joint Venture Success:
A Sino–U.S. Perspective

International joint ventures are important vehicles for multinationals expanding
into developing countries. There is widespread acceptance that there is often a
difference in perceptions of the determinants of the success of those joint ventures among the partner firms (Berg, Duncan, and Friedman, 1982; Peterson and
Shimada, 1978). Frequently unrealistic expectations concerning the potential of
the joint venture may lead to disappointment and to the eventual failure of the
joint venture. This issue is particularly important when forming a joint venture in
a developing country such as the People's Republic of China (PRC), where the
cultural differences compared with Americans are high. This study seeks to
assess the attitudes of Chinese managers about joint venture success, and to
compare these to the attitudes of American managers. Resulting management
issues are identified and the implications discussed.

Joint venture success

There is a growing body of literature addressing the key factors for joint venture
success (Harrigan, 1986; Killing, 1983). One explanation for success stems from
theories of competitive behavior that suggest that a joint venture will be viewed
as successful if it improves the competitive position of the parent firms
(Harrigan, 1985). Another perspective suggests that a joint venture will be
viewed as successful if the parent firm learns from its partner about technology,
routines, management expertise, etc. (Kogut, 1988). Other perspectives view
success as a function of the longevity or profitability of the joint venture. For
success, there must be evolving management structures and a commitment to
collaborate that leads to lasting complementarities (Lorange and Roos, 1987).
Thus, success is traditionally defined by assessing the parent's ability to prosper
from the relationship and also by the joint venture's viability.

One aspect of joint venture performance that is also treated at length in the

Inga S. Baird, Marjorie A. Lyles, and Robert Wharton are at Ball State University,
Muncie, IN. Shaobo Ji is at Dalian University of Technology, Dalian, PRC.

literature is lack of success or dissatisfaction with the venture. Satisfaction with the joint venture is often determined by the amount of conflict (or lack thereof) between the parents, the amount of control, changing goals, and structural issues (Killing, 1983; Kogut, 1988; Lyles, 1987).

From the literature, it is apparent that Chinese and American views of joint venture success differ. In the Chinese culture, there is a lack of separation between the business entity, the government, and the society. The joint venture is expected to serve all three stakeholders. Therefore, the Chinese want joint ventures with foreign partners in order to gain access to technology and foreign capital. They want the joint ventures to include a minimum of risk, to fit with traditional Chinese organizational structures, and to interface with governmental goals. Traditional Chinese organizational structures include a clan-like structure with a heavy emphasis on informal communication, patriarchal decision making, guaranteed pay, and egalitarian performance criteria based on the hierarchy (Baird, Lyles, and Wharton, 1989; Boisot and Child, 1988; Von Glinow and Teagarden, 1988).

In the American conception, a successful joint venture is profitable and continues to be competitive. Harrigan (1986) and Killing (1983) conclude that in successful joint ventures, there should be a participatory style of decision making, with the joint venture management having some say in the decision making. Rewards should be based on performance in meeting the goals. The ideal joint venture should allow for some conflict that encourages the presentation of alternative views, have a democratic structure, and allow individual initiative. It should be the result of two equal partners cooperating even when one partner may have more management control than the other (Harrigan, 1986; Killing, 1983).

This study focuses on the perceptions of American and Chinese managers about criteria associated with joint venture success. It is anticipated that their conceptualizations of an ideal joint venture and their expectations of the types of problems encountered will reflect their differing backgrounds.

Methodology

Sample

The sample included American and Chinese middle-level managers. The data were collected in 1988. Thirty Chinese managers and thirty-seven American managers participated. An attempt was made to match the two sample groups as closely as possible. The age and sex distribution of the groups were comparable, as were their years of administrative experience. However, the Chinese had somewhat fewer years of education.

The Chinese managers were attending a training seminar entitled "Science and Technology" in Dalian organized by the U.S. Department of Commerce.

They were from various provinces and represented governmental agencies and business enterprises that were concerned with technology development. All were practicing managers, having three to ten years of work experience, with job titles such as "administrator," "director," or "chief engineer." About 90 percent had some college education. Very few had any direct experience with joint ventures. The Chinese version of the survey instrument was administered while the managers were in a classroom, and they were instructed to answer it individually.

Subsequently, an English version of the survey was administered to thirty-seven American MBA students enrolled in a Midwestern, state-supported university. Most of the U.S. respondents were in managerial or supervisory positions, and had from two to ten years work experience. Only two had any direct experience with joint ventures.

Questionnaire

The questionnaire required the respondents to indicate their agreement or disagreement regarding items addressing joint venture management. The questions were translated into Chinese by a graduate student from the PRC, who had previously worked as a translator. The questionnaire was subsequently retranslated from Chinese back into English by a Chinese faculty member, and the translation was adjusted to correct any unclear statements. The Chinese version was rechecked in Dalian.

The survey includes three sections addressing the factors leading to success, descriptions of an ideal joint venture, and issues that would occur during an actual joint venture. Many items were selected from other questionnaires with acceptable reliability and validity, which had been administered to groups of Asian and American managers (Osborn and Baughn, 1988; Lyles, 1988). The first set of questions measures agreement on a five-point scale (1 = strongly agree; 5 = strongly disagree) with nine statements about the extent to which the respondents agreed that the factors lead to success. The second set consists of eighteen statements that relate to an ideal joint venture. The third section specifies issues that might arise in an actual joint venture. While the first two sets examine perceptions of an ideal joint venture, this section is designed to determine whether the respondents anticipate some of the problems that have been documented as common in joint ventures (Lyles, 1987). A Likert five-point scale (1 = little; 5 = very much) provided an indication of how strongly the respondents agreed or disagreed that they would have to deal with an issue during an actual joint venture.

Analysis

Chinese and American managers' attitudes were analyzed using *t*-tests to evaluate the differences between group means. One difficulty interpreting the results and in making comparisons between managers in the two countries is the marked "agree-

Table 1. Factors leading to successful joint ventures

	adjusted means		discriminant coefficient	rank	
	U.S.	PRC		U.S.	PRC
government support	5.00	1.88***	0.66	9	3
venture managers are fluent in the partner's language	3.79	5.00	0.12	7	9
joint strategic decision making regarding the venture	1.75	2.13	0.12	3	4
common goals	1.36	3.50**	−0.05	2	7.5
trust	1.00	1.00	0.14	1	1
mutual need	2.46	1.25**	0.38	5	2
well-developed reporting systems	3.12	3.34	0.18	6	6
high profits	4.24	3.50	0.42	8	7.5
familiarity with partner's business culture and customs	1.97	2.50	0.10	4	5

***p of $t \leq 0.001$
**p of $t \leq 0.01$
*p of $t \leq .05$
Scale: 1 = strongly agree; 5 = strongly disagree

ability" of the Chinese respondents to the first two sets of statements (the mean Chinese response to the nine items in question one was 1.55 with a standard deviation of 0.34; the U.S. mean for these same nine items is 2.22 with a 0.65 standard deviation). Therefore, a normalized figure was calculated for both countries to correct for any response bias. This involved subtracting the overall within-country mean for each subset of items from each individual score, and dividing that difference by the within-country standard deviation for that same set of items. Scores were then readjusted to fall within the original range of one through five.

For each set of questions, a discriminant function was calculated to establish the degree to which the included items could differentiate between the responses of U.S. and Chinese managers. Correlation coefficients with the overall discriminant function, presented in each figure, help to establish the ability of the individual items to distinguish between managers of either country. In addition, the average responses of managers in both countries were ranked according to their degree of agreement with each statement. Together with the adjusted means, these two measures help present a clearer picture of the differences between the two groups.

Results

Responses to the question dealing with factors leading to success, once the joint venture is started, showed several significant differences between Chinese and

American managers. Results presented in Table 1 show that both groups felt trust was very important to success, as was joint strategic decision making regarding the venture. However, managers in the PRC rated mutual need and government support as more necessary to success than did American managers, while U.S. managers saw common goals as more important than did the Chinese. Familiarity with the partner's business culture and customs, fluency in the partner's language, well-developed reporting systems, and high profits were less salient for both respondent groups.

When asked to describe the ideal joint venture, Chinese and American managers exhibited striking differences. As shown in Table 2, American managers envisioned the ideal joint venture as one where creativity, flexibility, and adaptability to change were encouraged. In contrast, Chinese managers viewed minimal risk of failure and the existence of a formal hierarchy of authority as descriptive of the ideal joint venture.

Both groups ranked highly the following attributes of an ideal joint venture: a formal system for measuring performance, significant raises and promotions for outstanding performance, superior's knowledge of employees' performance, and lots of informal communication. Chinese and Americans agreed that certain characteristics were less strongly associated with an ideal joint venture and perhaps associated with a problem joint venture. These included having to clear decisions with either parent corporation, repayment of the initial investment in five years, and disbanding the joint venture after ten years. While both groups disliked being obliged to follow orders coming down to them through the hierarchy, Chinese managers had a significantly more positive view of this requirement than did Americans. Also, the Chinese saw the foreign parent's provision of technology with the domestic firm contributing manufacturing as significantly more appealing than did the American respondents.

In reference to issues they would have to deal with in an actual joint venture, Chinese and Americans anticipate frequent problems relating to cultural misunderstandings, slow decision making, high costs, and personality conflicts. However, results in Table 3 demonstrate that the Chinese expect to have to deal with personality conflicts significantly more often than do Americans. Americans predicted that the major issue to be resolved in Chinese joint ventures involved the integration of manufacturing, marketing, personnel, and financial functions within the joint venture. They also felt they would have to handle problems of obtaining high-quality inputs less often than did the Chinese. This may reflect a lack of experience with international joint ventures on the part of the U.S. respondents.

Discussion

It is proposed that definitions of success, attributions of success to particular causes, and expectations of problems to be faced will affect the managers' be-

Table 2. Managing the "ideal joint venture"

	adjusted means		discriminant coefficient	rank	
	U.S.	PRC		U.S.	PRC
Major decisions must be cleared by the Chinese parent	3.50	4.21	0.01	13	16
Major decisions must be cleared by the foreign parent	3.46	4.39*	0.02	12	17
The foreign parent provides technology, Chinese provide manufacturing	4.14	2.07***	0.37	16	10
The foreign parent provides education & training	2.96	3.12	0.05	11	12
Written rules, procedures, and work instructions	2.32	1.85	0.15	7	8.5
There is a formal system of measuring performance	1.96	1.43	0.15	5	3
The venture has the authority to set its own budgets	2.46	1.76	0.17	8	7
The venture is flexible and adapting to change	1.18	2.33**	−0.09	2	11
Creativity is encouraged	1.00	1.85	−0.04	1	8.5
Superiors know whether employees are doing a good job	1.64	1.67	0.09	3	6
There is a lot of informal communication	1.87	1.12*	0.22	4	2
The venture strategy involves minimal risk of failure	4.09	1.00***	0.61	15	1
Significant raises and promotions are given for outstanding work	2.14	1.57	0.15	6	4.5
The main function of members is to follow orders that come down through the channels	4.82	3.76**	0.26	17	15
There is a system of peer reviews among the venture's managers	2.82	3.42	0.02	9.5	13
In the venture, a formal hierarchy of authority exists	2.82	1.57**	0.26	9.5	4.5
The venture will disband after 10 years	5.00	5.00	0.11	18	18
The venture will repay its initial investment within 5 years	3.59	3.48	0.09	14	14

***p of $t \leq 0.001$
**p of $t \leq 0.01$
*p of $t \leq .05$
Scale: 1 = strongly agree; 5 = strongly disagree

havior to the extent that each pursues certain goals, attends to certain causal factors, and focuses on solving certain problems. If respondents reflect the hopes and fears common to managers from their respective cultures with regard to joint

Table 3. Expected problems in an "actual joint venture"

	adjusted means		discriminant coefficient	rank	
	U.S.	PRC		U.S.	PRC
Integrating manufacturing, marketing, personnel, & financial functions	5.00	1.23***	0.75	1	10
Loss of technological knowledge	1.001	1.00	0.21	11	11
Lost competitive or market position	1.47	1.97	0.13	9	7
Mistrust of partner firms	1.85	1.45	0.24	8	9
Slow or delayed decision making	3.31	2.82	0.30	3	5
Conflict over the original agreement	1.39	2.25	0.14	10	6
Personality conflicts	2.54	5.00**	−0.00	4	1
Conflicting goals	2.01	1.50	0.28	7	8
Cultural misunderstandings	3.77	4.88	0.12	2	2
High costs	2.08	3.05	0.12	5.5	4
Obtaining high quality inputs	2.08	4.31*	0.00	5.5	3

***p of $t \leq 0.001$
**p of $t \leq 0.01$
*p of $t \leq .05$
Scale: 1 = little; 5 = very much

venture participation, some valid conclusions may be drawn regarding the potential for smooth cooperation and effective performance in Sino–American joint ventures.

Definitions of joint venture success

Results of this survey substantiate previous findings that longevity is a common basis for defining joint venture success. Both groups felt that disbanding the venture within ten years was not descriptive of the ideal joint venture. However, other characteristics, such as flexibility and existence of a formal hierarchy, found in this study to be related to the ideal joint venture, have not been discussed frequently in the literature. This may reflect respondents' individual or cultural ideals of what a work organization should be. Both groups thought the ideal successful joint venture would be characterized by good managerial appraisal systems and subsequent rewards for good performance. However, the basis for these rewards differed. Chinese felt that the ideal venture would be associated with minimal risk of failure as well as with the presence of a formal hierarchy and the safety it provides. In direct contrast, Americans envisioned success in a joint venture setting to be tied to creativity, flexibility, and innovation. Informal communications within the ideal joint venture would serve the Americans as a source of new ideas and as an early warning of problems. Informal communication to the Chinese is a source of information about the preferences, actions, and reactions of important authority figures. Thus, from the individual's perspective, the ideal or successful joint venture is one where managers can be rewarded for achieving goals meaningful in their culture.

Factors leading to joint venture success

Americans think that factors leading to joint venture success involve different but equal partners, knowledge about each other's culture and language, working together on an equal footing in conditions of trust to achieve common goals. Two independent partners joining to make strategic decisions and to pursue a common good was the basis of joint venture success. In contrast, Chinese managers think that a successful joint venture is based on shared dependency and mutual need (not mutual goals or contributions). Success in a joint venture is tied to the existence of a trusting, clan-like relationship, bowing to the authority of the government, but still able to cooperate in business decisions.

Expected problems in joint ventures

The two groups both felt that once the joint venture was launched, mistrust, conflicts over the original agreement, and conflicting goals would not have to be dealt with frequently. The major issues Americans felt would arise lay in the area of integration of various functions and cultural misunderstandings, personality conflicts, and slow decision making that would make the integration and operation of the joint venture difficult. The Chinese were apparently more sensitive than the Americans to other issues involving personality and cultural conflicts. Problems of slow decision making, cost concerns, and lack of quality inputs are endemic in China. The Chinese recognized they would have to deal with these issues more frequently than did the Americans.

Neither group was concerned about loss of technological, market, or competitive position. While this may be understandable for the Chinese, it may reflect a blind spot on the part of the Americans regarding the potential dangers of international joint ventures. The U.S. managers did indicate that the foreign partner providing technology and the domestic partner providing manufacturing was not ideal in a joint venture, but this may be associated with a desire to pursue common goals rather than a fear of losing a technological advantage.

Limitations and future research needs

Several limitations of this investigation must be acknowledged. First, few of these managers had any experience with international joint ventures, so that their responses may not reflect the actual definitions of joint venture success used by sophisticated firms, or accurately identify factors affecting joint venture success. Also, most of the managers in this study were successful managers who were selected by their organizations or supported by their firms for advanced management education, so that the results may not generalize to managers with more modest accomplishments. Third, the size of the sample groups triggers a number of concerns, e.g., would the results hold with larger groups? It may be that some of the results would change with managers from different backgrounds or representing different industries. Additional research is also needed to examine how managerial beliefs and expectations affect performance in a joint-venture setting.

Implications

Successfully implementing a joint venture, after all the papers are drawn up and signed, provides serious challenges to managers. For instance, careful attention must be paid to determining the basis on which success will be measured and rewards will be allocated. When one party defines success as creativity, flexibility, and integration of multiple functions, and the other defines it as risk avoidance, adherence to the hierarchy, and conflict avoidance, they will probably find themselves frequently working at cross purposes. Creating a common organizational culture and establishing shared goals for the joint venture must be attempted. This is more vital to joint venture success than cultural understanding (Lyles, 1988; Harrigan, 1986), because goals can also serve as a basis of measuring performance and allocating rewards.

Similarly, attention must be given to structuring the joint venture and determining the roles of each parent company, as well as the roles of managers. Issues such as equality, independence, the importance of the hierarchy, and the desired amount of flexibility will arise during the operation of the joint venture. If these problems can be resolved before they occur, conflict damaging to the performance of the venture can be avoided.

The finding that American managers were unthreatened by the chances of yielding technological or competitive advantage to a foreign partner indicates that American companies may have to be more assiduous in alerting their employees to the consequences of such moves. In addition, negotiators of a joint venture agreement probably ought to structure the venture in such a way that the chances of creating a competent new competitor are minimized, since the middle managers of the venture may not be alert to the dangers of unlimited sharing of technical and marketing knowledge with a partner. This problem may be particularly important in China, where there are limits set to the life span of a joint venture.

"Premarital counseling" for joint venture partners before implementation of the endeavor has been recommended by several authors (Harrigan, 1986; Lyles, 1987; Killing, 1983). In Sino–U.S.ventures, this may be particularly critical to success, because of the differing ideals, expectations of success and problems, and notions of causality that the parties bring to the venture.

Postscript

This survey was repeated with a second group of Chinese managers in Dalian during August 1989. Few significant changes were found in the responses of the 1988 group. However, concerns for the security of capital and profits (that were not dealt with on the questionnaire explicitly) may have been of increased importance in the Americans' criteria for joint venture success as a result of changes in the Chinese political scene during June 1989.

Acknowledgment

Special thanks are due to the United States Department of Commerce and to the Dalian University of Technology, for assistance in data collection.

References

Baird, I. S.; Lyles, M. A.; and Wharton, R. (1989) "Attitudinal Differences between American and Chinese Managers Regarding Joint Venture Management." Paper presented at the Academy of Management, Washington, D.C.

Berg, S. V.; Duncan, F.; and Friedman, P. (1982) *Joint Venture Strategies and Corporate Innovation.* Cambridge, MA: Oelgeschlager, Gunn & Hain.

Boisot, M., and Child, J. (1988) "The Iron Law of Fiefs: Bureaucratic Failure and the Problem of Governance in the Chinese Economic Reform." *Administrative Science Quarterly,* 33, pp. 507–527.

Harrigan, K. R. (1985) *Strategies for Joint Ventures.* Lexington, MA: Lexington.

———. (1986) *Managing for Joint Venture Success.* Lexington, MA: Lexington.

Killing, J. P. (1983) *Strategies for Joint Venture Success.* New York: Praeger.

Kogut, B. (1988) "Joint Ventures: Theoretical and Empirical Perspectives." *Strategic Management Journal,* 9, pp. 319–332.

Lorange, P., and Roos, J. (1987) "The Impact of National Differences on Cooperative Venture Formation Processes." Working Paper, Stockholm School of Economics, Institute of International Business.

Lyles, M. A. (1987) "Common Mistakes of Joint Venture Experienced Firms." *Columbia Journal of World Business,* 22, pp. 79–85.

———. (1988) "Learning among Joint Venture Sophisticated Firms." *Management International Review,* 28, pp. 85–98.

Osborn, R. N., and Baughn, C. C. (1988) "Role of Technology in the Formation and Form of Multinational Cooperative Arrangements." Working Paper, Wayne State University, Detroit, MI.

Peterson, R. B., and Shimada, J. Y. (1978) "Sources of Management Problems in Japanese–American Joint Ventures." *Academy of Management Review,* 3, pp. 796–804.

Von Glinow, M. A., and Teagarden, M. B. (1988) "The Transfer of Human Resource Management Technology in Sino–U.S. Cooperative Ventures: Problems and Solutions." *Human Resource Management,* 27, pp. 201–229.

JOHN FRANKENSTEIN

The Chinese Foreign Trade Environment

The Beijing Wind Revisited

The events of the spring of 1989 in China symbolize, in a paradoxical way, both the successes and the failures of China's decade-long "Second Revolution." That massive numbers of citizens from all walks of life in virtually every major city in the People's Republic rose up to express their dissatisfaction with the ineptitude of the Chinese authorities showed how far the process of reform had tempered fear and encouraged social relaxation. The repression that followed was a classic expression of the Chinese ruling circles' age-old obsession with absolute internal control, a shocking and painful reminder that, despite the regime's promises to depoliticize Chinese life, ultimately politics do indeed remain in command. One important aspect of that "Second Revolution" was, of course, economic. This involved the partial introduction of market forces throughout the economy and the devolution of management authority away from controlling central bureaucracies to the locality and enterprise levels. A salient part—but only a part—of these reforms was an opening of the Chinese economy to foreign trade and investment. This in turn was accompanied by a broad range of other economic measures, including the elaboration of a series of laws and regulations that formed the basis of an evolving commercial code, the expansion of investment zones, the enactment of special provisions to encourage foreign investment, and the proliferation of enterprises in the private and collective sectors.

As of late 1989, much of this economic reform package appears to be at risk: the regime talks of strengthening the central planning apparatus and reintroducing subsidies, of increased austerity measures, and of moves against the Chinese private sector. Just how these steps will affect the foreign business sector is unclear, but certainly a slowdown in the larger economy cannot but have a

John Frankenstein, Ph.D., is Associate Professor of International Studies, American Graduate School of International Studies, Glendale, AZ, and was Thunderbird Exchange Professor, University of International Business and Economics, Beijing, PRC. Starting January 1991 he will be at the Dept. of Management Studies, The University of Hong Kong.

negative effect. And how long a regime that is suspicious and critical of an indigenous private sector and that also blames its difficulties on malign foreign influences will keep its hands off foreign-invested enterprises is a matter of conjecture. (For a sampling of the variety of comment on the events see Chang, 1989; Goldman, 1989; Leung, 1989a; Lord, 1989; Renaud, 1989).

Furthermore, the foreign business community appears to be pulling back from China. The immediate response to the June events was to withdraw expatriate personnel, scale down operations, and reduce or freeze credit. While most foreign executives had returned by the end of the summer, the outlook for foreign business in China is not overwhelmingly bright. The political risk of doing business has grown: one not only has to take Chinese moves into account, but also must deal with increased trade restrictions imposed by Western governments. Private contacts report a mood of uncertainty and paralysis, a breaking off of well-developed contacts. "Things are just dead in the water," an experienced China trader told me in the fall of 1989.

Just the same, it would be a mistake to write off the last ten to fifteen years of foreign business experience. The Beijing political class is clearly in the first act of the succession crisis posed by the imminent passing of China's old revolutionary generation—the repression of June simply puts off the inevitable. Accordingly, we still have an interest in asking how the decade of reform changed the environment in which foreign business people were operating.

It was to explore these issues of change that we undertook a small business environment survey in the Beijing foreign business community in the summer of 1988. The survey replicated and refined one we conducted in 1984 (Frankenstein, 1986). In both cases, we asked to interview the chief representative of foreign firms (almost all of U.S. origin) operating in Beijing; we were particularly interested in talking with long-term players in the China market. To a certain degree, our findings report conditions that, for the short term at least, may no longer obtain. But as we reflect upon the past decade—"the ten almost years"—we can see an evolution toward greater Chinese understanding of and participation in the world trading system.

The respondents

Our 1984 data came from 26 business people of a variety of backgrounds, ranging from the law to engineering; 90 percent had been in business in China for over one year, and 50 percent for at least four years. Of the 26, 65 percent claimed to speak Chinese at the working level or better. Our 1988 group of 25 business people was roughly comparable in background, if a little more experienced: 84 percent had been in business in China at least two years, and 92 percent for at least six years. Of the 1988 group, 91 percent claimed to have at least social competence in spoken Chinese; 48 percent claimed professional competence. There was, we should note, one signal difference between the 1984 and 1988 groups. The earlier sample was made up entirely of persons of non-Chinese background. Half of the 1988 group were ethnic Chinese (although only a third of the group had been educated in the language, and just one-fifth were native speakers of Mandarin Chinese). Most were American citizens, some born in the United States, others in Taiwan or Hong Kong; others were employees of related firms in Hong Kong, and one was a PRC national. This is reflective of a change in the business atmosphere—a shift from making the deal and getting started, to implementation and making the deal work.

Still, given the small size of the groups, we would not force claims of strict representativeness or of rigorous statistical validity. But the results we obtained are consistent with other Chinese business environment studies (e.g., Campbell, 1986; Davidson, 1987; Hendryx, 1986; Pye, 1982, 1986). Furthermore, we would emphasize that our data come from face-to-face, structured interviews. While this methodology limited the range of our collection—availability and time were factors here—it ensured that we were able to deal directly with our target interview group.

The spiral model

Our earlier study suggested that Chinese business operating style, in both negotiations and in implementation, could be conceptualized as a spiral process characterized by continuous engagement, constant negotiations, and persistent attempts to deepen commitment.

This model carries with it a number of assumptions about the nature of Chinese business culture: that the Chinese put heavy stress on personal relationships; that contracts, far from being endpoints of an arms-length business process, are rather symbols of and starting points for those relationships; and that because personal relations in the Chinese setting are open-ended, business relationships are likewise open-ended. Other characteristics of the Chinese business setting and culture emerging from these studies include the use of shaming and blame-shifting techniques, political and dependency-establishing arguments, and a definitely non-North American approach to legal issues and time management. In sum, Chinese business culture and practices fit into the "high-context" paradigm suggested by the cross-cultural literature (see, for instance, Moran and Harris, 1982).

Negotiations

The spiral model is applicable to the negotiations process, an area of intense interest to the foreign business community. In both 1984 and 1988, we asked our interview groups to rank-order the most difficult negotiating issues they had encountered on a "difficult" to "easy to negotiate" scale. The results are given in Table 1.

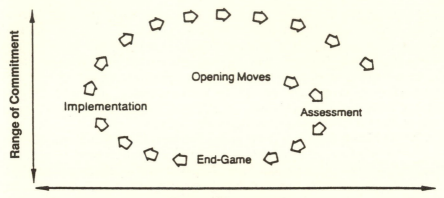

Figure 1. A spiral model of Chinese business practices and negotiating style

A comparison of these lists indicates an increased emphasis on operations and implementation—this is suggested by the relatively high ranking given to personnel issues and by the decline in items normally raised in negotiations, such as technology protection and valuation of joint-venture contributions. While other changes in the rank ordering are obvious, several points need to be made. First, while the list indicates relative difficulty of negotiating issues, only price and staff recruitment would appear to be significantly difficult issues; they both received, along with the matter of technology protection, low "easy to negotiate" scores. Of the other "difficult" issues, the matter of commodity inspections was termed by 52 percent of the group as "easy," as was staff training. These changes, particularly with respect to the valuation of joint venture contributions and technology protection, suggest that, as both foreign and Chinese sides learn more about each other, some kind of accommodation is occurring.

Money matters

However, price does remain a major sticking point. In 1984, one respondent noted that "price was the only consideration"; an American in China since 1978 observed that the "Chinese talk quality and buy price." Of our 1988 respondents, 76 percent agreed—36 percent "strongly"—with the statement that price and other up-front costs were uppermost in the minds of Chinese negotiators. Fifty-six percent felt that the Chinese with whom they had dealt did not understand Western cost structures and pricing practices (but one Hong Kong Chinese representing an international energy company suggested that this might be a ploy: "They just play dumb, that's all"). Still, this is a marked change from 1984, when 81 percent of our interviewees were of that opinion. Here we undoubtedly see some kind of learning and increased sophistication. The focus on immediate costs was bolstered by the finding that 72 percent of our 1988 group felt that the

Table 1.   Rank order of issues difficult to resolve (in order of difficulty)

1984	1988
1. Price	1. Price
2. Technology Protection	2. Recruitment and retention of Chinese staff
3. Valuation of joint venture contribution	3. Inspection of imported commodities
4. Training for Chinese staff	4. Training for Chinese staff
5. Delivery schedules	5. Payment schedules
6. Penalty clauses	6. Technology protection
7. Warranty protection	7. Profit repatriation
8. Determining technical specifications	8. Delivery schedules
	9. Valuation of joint venture contribution

Chinese did not have a good sense of life-cycle costs and that they did not understand the trade-offs among price, quality, reliability, and operational longevity. There are undoubtedly a host of reasons why price is key, not the least of which would be the generally recognized skill of Chinese negotiators. Anxiety over dealing with foreigners and about "getting burned" may also be factors.

But we would also suggest that foreign exchange issues emerge here. The Chinese insist that foreign joint ventures balance their foreign exchange expenditures, and a 1986 survey of Chinese trade officials and business people indicated that availability of foreign exchange was the single most important issue to consider in the establishment of foreign purchases (Frankenstein and Chao, 1988). Chinese ambivalence over debt and financing is another, related issue. Over half (52 percent) of our 1988 interview group indicated that the Chinese organizations with which they dealt relied on them to find sources of financing and foreign exchange to support business agreements. A manager for a U.S. company said that he was surprised by the complexity of the deals in which he was involved. He noted that "the ways of doing business were changing"—deals had "multiple attributes: price, foreign exchange, counter-purchase, transfer of technology." The upshot here is that foreign businesses, unless they hold enormous bargaining power, must be flexible in assisting their Chinese partners. A Hong Kong Chinese with extensive experience in the China trade remarked: "The reality is you can't push your Chinese partner. You have to lead him, give hints and talk business in personal terms. It's difficult to settle issues around a negotiating table."

In addition, almost half (48 percent) of our 1988 response group agreed that being prepared to engage in countertrade gave them a competitive advantage (although 26 percent disagreed). Just the same, countertrade has its problems: the manager of one U.S. firm that has done some counterpurchase noted that quality

and delivery of the countertrade goods were "problematic." A management consultant in the China trade for over ten years likewise was not very enthusiastic
about countertrade: "headaches and lots of talk." And a trader noted that as far as
he was concerned, "95 percent of countertrade deals have eventually fallen
through, with the Westerners getting burned."

Continuities: renegotiation, blame-shifting

If price remains a key concern, what about other features of the negotiating
environment? We found other continuities that suggested the persistence of the
spiral model; in fact, many of our percentages from 1984 matched our 1988
numbers. For instance, almost half of our 1988 group indicated that the Chinese
attempted to renegotiate signed contracts to their advantage (20 percent were
neutral on this issue, and 16 percent disagreed with this assessment; 50 percent
of the 1984 group also agreed with this proposition). On this matter, one Hong
Kong Chinese manager commented that he was struck by the "slowness of
decision making and the constant negotiations, before, during, and after the
contract." Fifty-two percent felt that the Chinese tended to shift the blame to the
Western side if difficulties were encountered (20 percent were neutral and 16
percent disagreed), and a similar percentage felt that the Chinese tended to link
international political issues with commercial negotiations. A Hong Kong Chinese working as an agency general manager commented on this last item: "I
couldn't agree with that more." (About half the 1984 group agreed here). Sixty
percent felt that China used its economic weakness as a bargaining ploy (20
percent disagreed; 67 percent of the 1984 respondents agreed). One manager, a
Hong Kong Chinese, was acerbic: "Chinese officials get away with presenting
China as a backward country. They use this as an excuse not to comply with
international standards and blow off [proper] documentation."

Continuities: technical information, time, and the center

Of the 1988 group, 72 percent felt that the Chinese demanded more technical
information than other international customers (in 1984, 60 percent agreed)—
this reflects not only the technology transfer focus of Chinese foreign trade but
also the Chinese concern about "getting burned" besides, perhaps, the cultural
imperative of establishing broad context and information matrices necessary for
decision making. And 64 percent were of the opinion that the Chinese still
controlled the timing and pace of negotiations, that is, they were able to manipu-
late the "home court advantage"; in 1984, the same percentage was of the same
opinion. A Hong Kong Chinese manager with considerable China trade experience noted that "all the time is on the Chinese side." An American executive
with a technology company commented: "The Chinese love it when people [they
are dealing with] do not live in China because they have to leave. If you live

here, you can say that you will be here as long as it takes. When you've got all the time in the world, that rattles them."

Decision time and the locus of decision making also appear to be related. This is partially reflected in the virtually even distribution of opinion within our 1988 group regarding speed of Chinese bureaucratic decision making: 32 percent agreed that it was faster at the center than at provincial levels, but 28 percent disagreed and 24 percent were neutral on the issue. In this connection, however, we should note that when we asked the 1988 group which levels of the bureaucracy they preferred to interact with, 81 percent chose the center. One manager said that he preferred to deal with the central authorities because "decisions can be made more directly." And a New York bank representative advised that a useful tactic was to "go up high, [because] then they help you contact the level you want." Thus while decentralization is a fact, clearly dealing with the center still has its advantages. As one manager remarked: "Why start at the municipal level and get cut off at the knees when it's the central government that has to give the approval anyway?"

Changes in negotiations

Still, our 1988 group noted a number of changes in the negotiating environment. Most importantly, 80 percent agreed that, over the past two years, negotiations had noticeably speeded up. Further, almost half agreed that the Chinese negotiators generally had a detailed understanding of the end use of the product or service. These, we would suggest, reflect the decentralization and opening up of the system: foreign business people can now get to technically competent and operationally minded end users, and are no longer restricted to dealing with bureaucrats and professional negotiators at the center. As a banker noted: "You have to be outside Beijing now much more than in the past."

A surprise: cold calls

The extent of decentralization was reflected in a surprising response we got to a question about the most effective mode of establishing contacts for new business. While most of our respondents indicated that they worked through Chinese foreign trade corporations, the central ministries, organizations like CITIC, and trade fairs, a small but significant percentage (24 percent) indicated that they had considerable success with making cold calls, and a few of our interviewees (16 percent) said that the contacts they had developed through cold calls were among the most useful and effective they had established in China. One manager in the food processing business said that he had developed good joint venture operations in provinces as disparate as Hunan and Gansu—he routinely makes cold call visits to the appropriate provincial authorities on his considerable travels. A trader based in Beijing noted, "Making cold calls is not taken negatively here in

China. I wouldn't do this anywhere else, but here I just walk in and talk to people. If for nothing else, they'll stop and listen to me because I'm a foreigner."

The law

One aspect of the reforms that has received much attention has been the development of a set of laws governing foreign trade matters. How successfully is China moving toward attaining the goals of achieving a rule of law rather than of men? The responses suggest that some progress has been made here. We asked our group if the Chinese adhered strictly to the trade laws or whether one could negotiate around them: 41 percent felt that the laws set a firm standard, but 36 percent disagreed and 16 percent were neutral on the matter; a management consultant noted that "when there's a will, there's a way [to get around laws]." And one trader with long experience pointed out that the Chinese, in his experience, "tried to get around rules that don't benefit them."

Fifty-two percent felt that the Chinese did not follow international standards of contract compliance, but rather applied a double standard, which has advantages for the Chinese side (only 8 percent disagreed); this, however, is down from the 69 percent of managers who in 1984 were of this opinion. At the same time, there was some ambiguity concerning Chinese reliance on international standards in areas in which Chinese laws are unclear: 39 percent of the 1988 interviewees felt that China did not follow such a standard, and only 13 percent concurred (35 percent were neutral, and the rest did not respond to the item).

Furthermore, despite the increased formalization of the business setting, it appears that the Chinese still tend to avoid formal processes to resolve disputes: 72 percent of the group felt that the Chinese preferred informal methods to formal arbitration procedures as a way of resolving disputes between business partners. As an executive with long experience in the technology trade pointed out, the Chinese, in these cases, prefer "friendly discussions—arbitration doesn't look good."

Still, there are indications that trade laws and provisions do have some effect: just under half—44 percent—of the group agreed that the passage of the "22 Provisions" in 1986, which was to encourage foreign investment in China, had led to a significant improvement in the Chinese investment climate. But one manager in our 1988 group said that while the 22 Provisions were a good statement of policy from the center, out in the provinces "you still have to deal with the local warlord."

"Old friends"

In sum, the responses indicate that the Chinese business climate is in transition; for every indication of change, on can find the persistence of older practices; for every "yes," there is a "but." For instance, 80 percent of the 1988 sample agreed that the authority of Chinese operational personnel such as factory managers had increased and that political interference from unit party secretaries had declined (a trend that, as of late 1989, may be reversed). At the same time, an equal percentage agreed that, despite the positive changes, there are still "too many bureaucratic hassles" to deal with. We should not expect this situation to be otherwise, nor should we expect China to evolve a business system that mimics the West. Indeed, the Chinese leadership does not appear to have a definition of that evolution—this writer has had extensive and entertaining conversations with Chinese intellectuals and managers over the meanings of "planned market socialism" and "socialism with Chinese characteristics." A useful question, however, is what salient features from past practice continue.

Personalism

A good number of the continuities we have mentioned above are based on the personalistic approach to relationship building that is so much a part of Chinese practice. As an eight-year veteran of the China business scene noted, "Personal relationships are more important than any other factor." Most China traders would agree: 70 percent of our 1988 group agreed that being "an old friend" gave a foreign company a competitive advantage (28 percent agreed "strongly," 8 percent disagreed). But being an old friend, one manager noted, simply means "that you get to see the guy the second time you call." And a consultant with eight years in the China trade noted that the specificity of contacts was important: being a *lao pengyou* ("old friend") is "very marginal. What's key is knowing the right people. Being an old friend doesn't mean that the Chinese give you jobs on a platter, and often you have five 'old friends' competing with you." Still, the right connections, a Hong Kong Chinese executive noted, are essential: not only do "you have to find a really reliable local partner" for joint projects, but you have to "build *guanxi*—personal relationships—with senior officials."

The plan and the state: still key

Another set of continuities is a product of the nature of the Chinese economic and political system. Despite all the structural reforms, the present Chinese leadership remains committed to maintaining a socialist order in which "public ownership" (that is to say, state control) is the norm. Not surprisingly, 80 percent of our 1988 group indicated that the seventh five year plan was an important and useful guide to doing business in China. A senior executive at a successful joint venture advised: "Tie into the five-year plan. [You have to] understand the investment environment, particularly the Chinese objectives." In 1984, an American trader said that knowing about the plan gave him "greater negotiating leverage—they're committed to buy what we sell." In 1988, a European manager with a technology firm noted that "the help of the government is key." With austerity now the watchword, and with planning making a comeback, foreigners will have to pay even closer attention to state pronouncements.

Indeed, despite the proliferation of laws, the state is the final arbiter. A Chinese lawyer who represents Western firms in Beijing said that what his clients least understood about doing business in China was that, since the economy was under state control, the state could legitimately intervene in any business deal at any time under any pretext.

Lessons learned: dealing with uncertainty

This mix of old and new, the effect of incomplete learning and accommodation on both sides, results in perceptions of ambiguities. In 1984, one manager noted "the absolute difficulty of pinpointing who makes decisions." The bureaucracy was a problem—an executive in 1984 mentioned problems with "multiple jurisdictions" and competing interests in the Chinese bureaucratic setting. Their feelings were perhaps best summed up in a comment offered to us by an American lawyer in Beijing, who remarked on "the general sense of uncertainty and vagueness of the Chinese system. You think something is going to be a problem and it's not, and vice versa." These comments were echoed in 1988. One executive characterized business in China as follows: "Things can be so poorly communicated, and then one day [they go] though like wildfire. There's no standard for action, it's a roller coaster of highs and lows." Most of our respondents would agree with the management consultant who, when asked what surprised her about doing business in China, answered, "Nothing—anything can happen." Another veteran consultant responded: "I wouldn't say there is anything that surprises me. I've been here long enough to know anything can happen." And a businessman in China for eight years remarked stoically, "surprises always come."

Lessons learned: commonplaces of the China trade

Other comments stressed what we might call the commonplaces of the China trade: the need for preparation, planning, the long-term view, and understanding of the general business climate. One manager noted that in China there were "no overnight successes. Even IBM and American Express couldn't do it overnight—that should tell you something: do your homework." A Hong Kong accountant advised that one had to "understand the bureaucracy and the decision-making process. You had to understand with whom you are dealing and what authority he may have." Indeed, rank and hierarchy remain important in the Chinese trade: 68 percent of our interview group agreed that the Chinese were highly rank-conscious and that if difficult issues arose that required decisions from top Chinese management, it was essential that Western top executives be personally involved.

Costs were an issue as well. A Hong Kong Chinese working for an American firm noted, "beware of your overhead—very expensive." Another termed his overhead costs "astronomical." "Do your homework, know your costs," was the advice of another manager. The need for straight—and hard—thinking was also an issue for our 1988 group: "Don't take things at face value," an American technology manager suggested. "Double check thoughts and assumptions—look deeply for hidden costs."

A number of other difficulties were scored beyond frustrations with timing and the bureaucracy. Several of our respondents noted that they had to deal with numerous visits from high-ranking home office visitors. At the same time, they had difficulties making the home office understand the real situation in China. A banker noted,

> [There are] two axes [in doing business in China]: 'X'—You and your customers; your willingness to deal with ambiguity and to wait; not to have clear answers to questions vitally important to your corporation. 'Y'—You must manage your relationship with your boss and your head office—they don't understand your environment . . . help them understand your side of the story.

Surviving, coping, succeeding

In sum, as one consultant suggested, "You're not going to tell anybody anything new by telling [them] it's tough to do business here." At the same time, our 1988 response group did suggest ways to survive, cope, and perhaps succeed. A very experienced senior executive from the U.S. said, "Take it a day at a time. Don't lose your sense of humor. Do everything to mutual benefit." A Hong Kong Chinese urged patience, understanding of the local culture, and the need to "be persistent . . .never give up!" And an American working for a trading company advised "Do very, very good market research before coming here. Have enough working capital to stay for a long time without recovering costs. Make sure that key staff has good understanding of language, bureaucracy, and a good understanding of the business of the company."

Finally, our group was sensitive to the numerous pluses in the Chinese scene. An American noted that he was surprised that the positive changes had been sustained; he was encouraged by the "speed of change in the last decade. [It's been] accelerating over the past ten years." And despite the tales of corruption and opportunism, an engineer with eight years' work experience in China volunteered that he was taken with the "high level of professional and personal integrity of the Chinese."

The present future

As we have noted above, these findings underline the transitional nature of an evolving business climate. There are few if any surprises here. Certainly aspects of the spiral model remain very much in place; despite the reforms, Chinese business behavior remains difficult for the foreign business person to deal with. In sum, we can see structural change, but also constancy in behavior in the Chinese business environment.

But economic moves prompted by the recent political events appear to have successively dampened the rate of change. Despite state council assurances that the fall 1988 "rectification" would not affect foreign investment, some foreign-backed projects in construction and the hotel industry have been stopped (a small illustration of the importance of understanding the five-year plan, which gives scant if any priority to such undertakings—see Foreign Broadcast Information Service, 1988). More importantly, it is clear that the credit crunch is affecting the ability of some joint ventures to continue to sell into the China market, and, perhaps more important, the cutbacks have affected the ability of local Chinese enterprises to supply joint ventures—this may become crucial indeed, as many joint ventures require local content (see Ignatius, 1989).

Indeed, in private conversations in early 1989 with business people and knowledgeable observers of the foreign business scene in Beijing, one heard of "malaise" and increasing concerns about the long-term viability of the China trade under existing circumstances of austerity and cutbacks. The events of June 1989 and later policy pronouncements have only served to reinforce these concerns. Unofficial early reports from a November 1989 central committee plenum suggest a return to the Stalinist orthodoxies of central planning and political centralization. New investment, including non-plan foreign investment, will apparently be discouraged, and foreign trade dealings (formerly decentralized to the locality and enterprise levels, will evidently revert back to the centralized state foreign corporations. *The Wall Street Journal* quoted a Chinese economist familiar with the plans: "A single theme prevails in the documents—centralization, politically and economically. The plenum officially marks the beginning of the undoing of China's decade-long economic reform" (Leung, 1989b; see also do Rosario, 1989). At the same time, there are indications of potentially explosive provincial and bureaucratic resistance to Beijing's attempts to reassert its dominance (see, for instance, Tyson, 1989). Thus, as of this writing, China's business climate is cloudy, and the forecast is for continuing unsettled conditions.

Postscript

In the year since the crackdown around Tiananmen Square, those "unsettled conditions" have reflected themselves in a plunge in Western business activity in China, a serious erosion of foreign business confidence, and an increasingly difficult business environment. These are shown in both the numbers and in more impressionistic reporting from the People's Republic.

For instance, official Chinese statistics indicate that the value of foreign investment contracts finalized in the last quarter of 1989 (about $250 million) was down by a factor of ten from the $2.5 billion signed the previous quarter. Foreign investment in the first quarter of 1990 reached about $800 million, about half that of the first quarter of the previous year. U.S. investment, which reached $348 million for the first six months of 1989, was valued at only $48 million in the first quarter of 1990; reports indicate that continuing outside investment is in small deals. Exports have grown somewhat, but imports for January–April 1990 have declined sharply—by almost 20 percent (WuDunn, 1990; Delfs, 1990).

Not only has activity slowed, but apparently the climate has also hardened on both sides. Business people speak of disappointments, tougher negotiating stances, and hard times. Conflicts are now more apt to be taken to formal arbitration. An experienced trade lawyer, quoted in *The New York Times*, says "problems that were swept under the rug before are now becoming conflicts" (WuDunn, 1990). Indeed, it seems that one of the major costs of the Chinese retrenchment and crackdown has been a loss of international goodwill, something the Deng regime had been quite successful in cultivating. Even the usually upbeat *China Business Review* remarked that "Disillusionment carries a high cost for China" (Brecher, 1990).

To be sure, much of the current foreign trade slowdown can be attributed to the economic retrenchment and recentralization implemented in late 1988. While those moves cut inflation, they also led to a decline in industrial output, productivity, and demand (see Delfs, 1990). But certainly the events of 1989, the continuing atmosphere of repression, and officially inspired xenophobia has added substantially to the present disenchantment.

We cannot deny that on the international scene there are some signs of easing tensions. More than twenty years after Indonesia's communists, aided and abetted by China, mounted a bloody but failed uprising, Djakarta and Beijing are reestablishing diplomatic relations. In June 1990, at the biggest meeting of its kind to date, some 600 businessmen from Taiwan met in Beijing to explore opportunities on the mainland. As of this writing, China has kept its most favored nation status in trade with the United States. But internally, the pressure continues. The high profile, token releases of persons detained after June 3–4, 1989, and even the safe passage to exile given to Fang Li-Zhi and his wife Li Shu-Xian in June 1990, only underline the manipulative nature of the current regime.

The Chinese authorities may be trying to get the Chinese economic engine running more smoothly through loosened credit and an easing of attacks on the private sector; they may even be attempting to ease foreign fears by modifying the Joint Venture Law (see Delfs, 1990; Robertson and Chen, 1990). But the consensus of observers abroad and in the field appears to be that it will be a while before there is another Beijing spring.

Acknowledgments

The author would like to acknowledge the assistance and enthusiasm of the 1988 Thunderbird China Project team in data collection: Janet Almroth, James Black,

Greg Gallup, Amy Konvolinka, Janice Lin, Jeff McCorkle, Theo Miller, Jonathan Mudge, Tom Newman, and Tom O'Sullivan. We also thank the busy executives who took time out of their schedules to meet with us.

References

Brecher, Richard. (1990) "The End of Investment's Wonder Years." *China Business Review*, January/February, pp. 27ff.

Campbell, Nigel. (1986) *China Strategies: The Inside Story*. University of Manchester and University of Hong Kong, 1986.

Chang, Maria Hsia. (1989) "The Meaning of the Tiananmen Incident." *Global Affairs*, Fall 1989, pp. 12–35.

Cheng, Elizabeth. (1990) "Goodbye, Cruel World: Why Foreign Investors See China as a Gamble." *Far Eastern Economic Review*, January 18, p. 40.

Davidson, William H. (1987) "Creating and Managing Joint Ventures in China." *California Management Review*, Summer 1987, pp. 77–94.

Delfs, Robert. (1990) "Belt Loosening." *Far Eastern Economic Review*, June 14, p. 56.

do Rosario, Louise. (1989) "Three Years' Hard Labour." *Far Eastern Economic Review*, November 30, 1989, pp. 68–69.

Foreign Broadcast Information Service. (1988) *China Daily Report*, Oct. 28, 1988. "State Council Spokesman Holds News Conference, Warns on Future of Joint Ventures."

Frankenstein, John. (1986) "Trends in Chinese Business Practice: Changes in the Beijing Wind." *California Management Review*, Fall 1986, pp. 148–60.

Frankenstein, John, and Chao, C. N. (1988) "Decision Making in the Chinese Foreign Trade Administration." *Columbia Journal of World Business*, Fall 1988, pp. 35–40.

Goldman, Merle. (1989) "Vengeance in China." *New York Review of Books*, November 9, pp. 5–9.

Hendryx, S. (1986) "The China Trade: Making the Deal Work." *Harvard Business Review*, July/August 1986, pp. 75 ff.

Ignatius, Adi. (1989) "Joint Ventures in China Hobbled by Beijing's Severe Credit Policy." *Asian Wall Street Journal Weekly*, April 3, 1989, p. 21.

Leung, Julia. (1989a) "Foreign Companies Brace for Plunge in Trade with China." *Asian Wall Street Journal Weekly*, October 9, pp. 1–2.

———. (1989b) "Retreat from Reform: Central Committee Sets Plan to Reassert Control over Major Sectors of Economy." *Asian Wall Street Journal Weekly*, December 4, p. 18.

Lord, Winston. (1989) "China and America: Beyond the Big Chill." *Foreign Affairs*, Fall 1989, pp. 1–26.

Moran, Robert, and Harris, P. (1982) *Managing Cultural Synergy*. Houston: Gulf.

Pye, Lucian. (1982) *Chinese Commercial Negotiating Style*. Boston: Oelgeschalger, Gunn & Hain.

———. (1986) "The China Trade: Making the Deal." *Harvard Business Review*, July/August 1986, pp. 74 ff.

Renaud, Bertrand. (1989) "Economic Reforms and Contradictions." *The World & I*, October 1989, pp. 76–85.

Robertson, Dario F., and Chen, Xiaokang. (1990) "New Amendments to China's Equity Joint Venture Law: Changes Unlikely to Stimulate Foreign Investment." *East Asian Executive Reports*, April, pp. 9–12.

Tyson, James L. (1989) "China Puts Brakes on Reforms." *Christian Science Monitor*, December 6, p. 4.

WuDunn, Sheryl. (1990) "Foreigners in China Feel Business Slip." *International Herald Tribune*, June 5, pp. 9, 13.

Betty Jane Punnett and Ping Yu

Attitudes toward Doing Business with the PRC

A Comparison of Canadian and U.S. Companies

The People's Republic of China (PRC) opened its doors to the outside world, and this resulted in a rush by foreign businesses to get a foothold in what was becoming recognized as a major emerging market. A population of over one billion, a rapidly developing economy, and undersupplied markets clearly provide many opportunities for North American businesses; in fact, the PRC has been described as "the last enormous underdeveloped market left in the world" (*Canadian Business*, July 1986, p. 16). The many opportunities that exist can be seen by examining the PRC government's officially announced priorities of economic development in the seventh five-year plan (*China Market*, January 1987).

Included were:

- Importation of advanced technologies and equipment from abroad for the priority sectors of energy, telecommunications, and raw materials;
- importation of generating equipment for thermal, hydro, and nuclear power;
- enhancement of mining and mechanization;
- solutions for transportation difficulties;
- development of natural gas and oil reserves;
- development of the chemical industry;
- focus on metallurgy;
- improvement of the quality of basic components in the machinery and equipment industries;
- enhancement of the quality and variety of electronic products;
- acceleration of development of large-scale integrated circuits, computers, microelectronics technology, optical fiber, program-controlled telephones, and satellite communications;
- development of light industry, textiles, food processing, pharmaceuticals, and other industries to meet the needs of the people.

The authors are at the University of Windsor, Ontario, Canada.

The PRC government was encouraging investment in the sectors of energy, machine-building, electronics, light industry, textiles, agriculture, animal husbandry, fishing, and "productive projects" (manufacturing and mining). These were being encouraged through a variety of incentives (*China Market*, May 1987). The opportunities presented by China's open door policy should be attractive to both U.S. and Canadian businesses. Trade and investment figures suggest, however, that U.S. companies were relatively aggressive in pursuing the Chinese market, but that, somewhat surprisingly, Canadian companies were less aggressive (Punnett and He, 1988).

Canada's lower level of involvement with China is surprising for several reasons. First, foreign trade in general is more important to Canada's economy (28.8 percent of GNP in 1985) than it is to the U.S. economy (7.0 percent) (National Accounts Statistics, 1987); therefore, one might expect Canadian businesses to be more aggressive in pursuing this new foreign market rather than less aggressive. Second, in many ways Canada and China would seem like good business partners. The competitive advantage of Canada's large firms lies in "their efficient management of mature and resource-based product lines, as well as their effective marketing of these products" (Rugman and McIllveen, 1985, p. 5), and Canadian firms have a knowledge-based advantage in communication, transportation, and power development. These are advantages that appear to match Chinese economic development priorities. Canadian and American business people have much in common, and the cultures of the two nations are relatively similar (e.g., Hofstede, 1981; Jackowsky, Slocum, and McQuaid, 1988). Canadians have, however, been described as more conservative and risk-averse than their American counterparts (Hardin, 1974; Lipset, 1968); this may explain a more cautious attitude toward the opportunities represented by the PRC.

The purpose of the present study is, first, to examine the attitudes of U.S. and Canadian executives toward opportunities in the PRC, and to explore the reasons for U.S. companies' greater involvement in the Chinese market than their Canadian counterparts. There is a substantial recent body of literature on the PRC; this research includes references to both Canada and the United States, but does not specifically compare attitudes in the two countries toward doing business in the PRC. In addition, the relative importance of various issues to executives from both countries are examined. Previous research has identified both opportunities and drawbacks to doing business with the PRC, but the relative importance of various issues to the business community has not been clearly delineated.

There were several reasons for undertaking this survey. First, results of a survey of this kind can provide information for the PRC government; the information gathered in such a survey can be used to improve efforts to attract appropriate trade and investment. The results should also be of interest to the U.S. and Canadian governments; by identifying the concerns of their respective companies, the home governments can improve their efforts to encourage trade with, and investment in, the PRC. Finally, companies considering doing business with the PRC, as well as those already involved in such business, can benefit from learning of the concerns of others.

In order to identify issues to include in the survey, the literature on doing business with the PRC was reviewed, and a list of issues suggested as important was compiled. Both positive and negative issues were identified as potentially of importance to companies considering or currently doing business with the PRC. The major issues discussed in the literature were classified into eight categories. These categories were not mutually exclusive, and by no means all inclusive, but they were reasonably distinct and incorporated the issues identified most often as important. The eight categories were: attractiveness of the Chinese market (*China Market*, January, May 1987; Hendryx, 1986; Wang, 1986; Xu, 1985), Chinese government incentives (*Business International*, October 27, 1986; Ho, 1984), home government incentives (Beamish, 1984), Chinese restrictions (Davidson, 1987; Zamet and Bovarnick, 1986), economic differences (Ho and Huenemann, 1984; *Business Asia*, February 10, 1986), business practice differences (Ruggles, 1983; Zamet and Bovarnick, 1986), cultural differences (Hendryx, 1986; Tung, 1986), and infrastructure (personal interview, 1988).

These overall categories were further subdivided into a number of more specific issues as follows:

1. *Chinese market:* size, costs, management availability, skilled labor availability, materials/energy availability.

2. *Chinese government incentives:* tax holidays, duty-free imports, exclusive rights, provision of services, dispute settlement.

3. *Home government incentives:* loans, feasibility financing, tax incentives.

4. *Chinese restrictions:* foreign exchange, capital repatriation, countertrade requirements, location requirements.

5. *Economic differences:* Centrally planned economy, government involvement in business, government-determined prices, government placement of labor.

6. *Business practice differences:* decision making, negotiating style, inexperience with the West, limited choice of suppliers, limited credit, limited ability to hire and fire, lack of control of technology.

7. *Cultural differences:* lifestyle, language, religion, food, attitude toward foreigners.

8. *Infrastructure:* transportation availability, communication availability, banking availability, information availability, wholesale–retail links.

Research design

The general categories identified, as well as the more specific questions, were discussed with academic colleagues familiar with the PRC as well as with corpo-

Table 1. Respondents' rankings of issues

Canadian respondents' rankings

issues	percent ranking as								
	1	2	3	4	5	6	7	8	*
Chinese restrictions	21	33	9	0	12	3	12	0	9
home govt. incentives	3	15	12	9	0	21	12	21	6
Chinese incentives	6	9	9	18	9	12	12	21	3
cultural differences	3	6	0	6	12	15	15	33	9
economic differences	3	0	15	9	21	18	15	9	9
business practices	6	18	15	21	12	9	6	3	6
infrastructure	3	9	24	15	15	12	12	3	6
Chinese market	52	6	15	9	9	0	6	0	3

U.S. respondents' rankings

issues	percent ranking as								
	1	2	3	4	5	6	7	8	*
Chinese restrictions	25	63	19	10	6	8	1	1	4
home govt. incentives	0	3	8	8	6	10	18	44	5
Chinese incentives	1	16	13	10	15	19	14	8	5
cultural differences	0	0	4	10	5	19	30	28	5
economic differences	5	15	8	15	14	18	13	8	6
business practices	9	14	21	14	32	9	6	1	4
infrastructure	4	15	18	21	14	9	11	4	5
Chinese market	54	8	6	8	13	5	3	1	4

* missing values

rate executives. The purpose of these discussions was to ensure that respondents would find the issues meaningful. Following these discussions, a survey instrument was designed. The questionnaire consisted of two parts; part one identified the general categories and asked respondents to rank these in order of importance; part two broke each major category into subcategories and asked respondents to rate the importance of each on a five-point scale from very important to unimportant. The first part was intended to force respondents to think of the relative importance of each issue, the second part was intended to examine each issue in greater depth. The questionnaire was administered through a mail survey to Canadian and American businesses as follows:

Canadian sample: Canadian firms that had expressed an interest in China were identified from the Globe and Mail's International Business Section; those listed in the Canadian Business Directory were then contacted by mail. A covering letter asking for participation in the project was written to the chief executive officer of each company. A total of 57 questionnaires were mailed, 4 were returned unanswered, 33 were returned completed and usable.

U.S. sample: U.S. firms interested in the PRC were identified from a list of members of the National Council for U.S.–China Trade; those listed in industrial directories were then contacted by mail with a similar covering letter. A total of 160 questionnaires were mailed, 12 were returned unanswered, 80 were completed and usable.

The subject population had all expressed an interest in China, although not all were actively conducting business in the PRC; this was felt to be an appropriate group to survey because they would have given some thought to issues that could arise and thus would be able to answer the questionnaire in a meaningful manner.

Results and discussion

The 33 questionnaires completed by the Canadian sample represent a 62 percent response rate. The 80 completed by the U.S. sample represent a 50 percent response rate. This is a relatively high response rate for a mail survey. While non-respondents' views cannot be examined, it is likely that non-respondents were those who were less interested in the topic or felt that they could not respond meaningfully. If this is correct, then the responses to this survey should have given an accurate picture of the concerns that interested companies have, relative to doing business with the PRC. The results from part one of the mail survey are presented in Table 1 in the form of percentages of respondents ranking a particular category in a particular position from one to eight (one is most important, eight is least important).

The attractiveness of the PRC market was clearly very important to both sets of respondents; 52 percent of Canadian respondents ranked this as number one and 54 percent of U.S. companies felt it to be most important. Also of high importance were PRC government restrictions. Of the Canadians, 21 percent ranked this as number one and 33 percent as number two; U.S. respondents considered this even more important, with 25 percent ranking it number one and 63 percent ranking it number two. At the other extreme, cultural differences appear to be considered of least importance. Of Canadian respondents, 33 percent ranked this as least important, and 28 percent of U.S. respondents ranked cultural differences last.

These responses can be grouped in terms of rankings from 1 through 4 (more important) versus rankings 5 through 8 (less important) (see Table 2). These groupings, presented below, are particularly useful for comparative purposes. A χ^2 analysis of these responses for the two groups suggests some significant differences in how the two groups view doing business with the PRC (critical χ^2, $\alpha = 0.05$, is 3.84). Responses regarding Chinese restrictions ($\chi^2 = 4.97$) and home government incentives ($\chi^2 = 5.44$) were significantly different for the two groups. U.S. respondents were relatively more concerned about restrictions, and

Table 2. Comparison of respondents' rankings

issue	Canada 1 – 4	U.S.	Canada 5 – 8	U.S.
Chinese market	82%	75%	15%	21%
Chinese restrictions	*63%	80%	36%	16%
business practices	60%	57%	30%	39%
China's infrastructure	51%	57%	42%	38%
Chinese incentives	42%	40%	55%	55%
home govt. incentives	*39%	17%	60%	77%
economic differences	27%	43%	63%	51%
cultural differences	15%	13%	75%	81%

Note: totals are less than 100% because of non-responses; * indicates significant difference in response, critical $\chi^2 = 3.84$, $\alpha = 0.5$.

Canadians were relatively more interested in home government incentives.

These rankings indicate that, overall, the market is the major attraction for both groups; it is certainly not surprising that both groups ranked this as number one because the large untapped market is a prime reason for doing business with the PRC. Restrictions, business practices, and infrastructure are major concerns; incentives and economic differences are viewed as relatively less important; while cultural differences are seen as unimportant. Canadians see market opportunities as even more attractive than their U.S. counterparts, and Americans are more concerned about economic differences (these last differences were not statistically significant).

These differences suggest a possible explanation for Canadians' less aggressive attitude toward entering this market. Canadian government incentives appear to be a somewhat important aspect of their decision making relative to the PRC and incentives may not be readily available (Punnett and He, 1988). The Americans, in contrast, while concerned about Chinese government restrictions, may believe that there are ways to deal with them.

The means from part two of the survey were examined. An ANOVA (analysis of variance) was first performed for each set of items to determine if there were any statistically significant differences between the responses of the two groups. In six of the eight cases, the F-ratio was significant at the α 0.05 level or less. There was no significant difference in how the two groups viewed the market and infrastructure. T-tests were performed on the individual items, where F was significant, to identify where the differences between the two groups lay. Table 3 presents those factors that were found to be significantly different between the two groups.

In examining these differences, it is important to consider practical signifi-

Table 3. Differences In Canadian and U.S. responses

	U.S.	Canada	
Chinese restrictions (F=3.9)			
countertrade requirements	3.8	3.4	t = 2.02
home govt. incentives (F=10.2)			
loans	2.8	3.6	t = 3.05
feasibility financing	2.7	3.6	t = 5.04
Chinese incentives (F=10.1)			
duty-free imports	4.0	3.5	t = 2.99
provision of services	3.9	3.6	t = 2.7
cultural differences (F=9.7)			
language	3.1	3.6	t = 3.3
economic differences (F=9.7)			
central planned economy	3.7	3.9	t = 2.5
govt. placement of labor	4.2	3.6	t = 2.63
business practices (F=8.2)			
decision-making differences	3.9	4.2	t = 2.29
negotiating style differences	3.7	4.1	t = 2.84
inexperience with the West	3.5	3.9	t = 3.82
limited ability hire/fire	4.0	3.5	t = 4.1
loss of control of technology	4.3	3.4	t = 3.05

cance as well as statistical significance. The issue of practical significance is a subjective one but it seems reasonable to suggest that responses that are different by at least 0.5 (e.g., 3.5 vs. 4.0) are in some sense practically different, i.e., this level of difference can be interpreted meaningfully. Some responses that show up as statistically different (see Table 3) are different by a smaller fraction than this; these are reported in the table but will not be discussed here as representing meaningful differences.

American respondents appear to be more concerned about Chinese government involvement in business than their Canadian counterparts. This can be seen in the U.S. mean rating of lack of control of technology at 4.3 (vs. 3.4 for Canadians), limited ability to hire and fire at 4.0 (vs. 3.5), and government placement of labor at 4.2 (vs. 3.6). On a quite separate issue, Americans responded that duty-free imports were more important (4.0) than did the Canadians (3.5). Canadian respondents seem to be more interested in home government incentives; they rated both loans and feasibility financing at 3.6, while American respondents rated these 2.8 and 2.7, respectively. On a separate issue, Canadian respondents rated language (3.6) as relatively more important than did their American counterparts (3.1).

Identification of the most important issues to each group (see Table 4) is also

Table 4. Most Important Issues

specific issue

top twelve Canadian responses	*mean*
foreign exchange control	4.7
availability of communication	4.6
availability of transportation	4.6
market size	4.4
differences in decision making	4.2
capital repatriation limitations	4.2
differences in negotiation styles	4.1
availability of information	3.97
government determined prices	3.97
operation costs	3.9
inexperience with the West	3.9
central planned economy	3.9

top twelve U.S. responses	*mean*
foreign exchange control	4.7
capital repatriation limits	4.4
control of technology	4.3
government determined prices	4.3
market size	4.3
availability of communication	4.2
government placement of labor	4.2
government involvement	4.1
tax holidays	4.1
availability of transportation	4.03
duty free imports	4.01
limited ability hire/fire	4.01

Note: 5 = very important, 4 = important, 3 = neutral, 2 = little importance, and 1 = unimportant.

helpful in identifying both similarities and differences in their attitudes toward doing business with the PRC (5 represents a response of "very important," 4 "important," 3 "neutral," 2 "little importance," and 1 "unimportant").

Canadian and U.S. respondents both rated foreign-exchange controls as most important (no. 1); in both groups, communication and transportation availability, capital repatriation limitations, government-determined prices, and market size were included among the top twelve considerations.

U.S. respondents were generally more concerned with Chinese government involvement in operations—including government control of technology, placement of labor, tax holidays, duty-free imports, and a limited ability to hire and fire among their top twelve concerns. Canadian respondents, on the other hand, appeared to be more concerned with differences in management practices, including differences in decision making, differences in negotiating styles, availability of information, inexperience with the West, and a centrally planned economy among their top twelve concerns. Canadians also mentioned costs of operation in the PRC as a fairly important concern while U.S. respondents did not.

These differences suggest another possible explanation for the Americans being more aggressive in pursuing opportunities in the PRC than the Canadians. Some of the concerns identified as being more important to the American respondents appear to be more concrete than those identified by Canadian respondents; they may, therefore, be seen as being easier to overcome. Some issues important to Canadians, such as "differences in decision making," are more abstract and may be seen by Canadians as a greater barrier to effective interactions.

Of least importance to both groups are religion and food; location requirements and local competition are also of little concern, and lifestyle in general is considered of little importance. Overall, cultural differences are considered unimportant by both sets of respondents.

The differences between the Canadian and U.S. respondents can probably be explained by general differences in attitudes as well as differences in company characteristics. As noted earlier, Canadians are generally considered more conservative and risk-averse than their American counterparts (Hardin, 1974); this would explain a more cautious attitude toward the opportunities presented by the PRC, as well as greater concern for differences in business practices. Canadians are also more accustomed to government controls (Hardin, 1974) and therefore may view these as less important; Americans, on the other hand, prefer to avoid government controls (Hardin, 1974) and therefore view these as a particularly important issue.

The Canadian companies that responded to the survey were smaller than the responding American companies, and, among those presently doing business in the PRC, there was less involvement than among the American companies, i.e., the majority of the Canadian companies had sales of under $200 million in the previous year, whereas the majority of the U.S. companies had sales of over $200 million; the majority of Canadian companies identified only one type of activity with the PRC, whereas the majority of U.S. companies identified two or more. This is not surprising because it reflects more general differences found between U.S. and Canadian organizations. The difference in size and activities of the organizations may explain some of the differences in their attitudes. Smaller organizations are more likely to need home-government support to consider entering a market such as the PRC, and they may be less experienced internationally, and, therefore, more concerned about different ways of doing business. Larger organizations with integrated activities may be more concerned about government controls and interference because this can affect more than just local operations.

The smaller Canadian organizations are likely to perceive the attractiveness of the Chinese market as particularly important, relative to their current operations, but its sheer size as less important because they would expect to capture only a small portion of such a market. The larger American organizations may see the PRC as only one of the many markets but its size as very important because they might expect to supply a large portion of it.

Conclusions and suggestions

The response rate was relatively high for both groups; this suggests that doing business in China continues to be a topic of interest to many companies. The reasons given for viewing China as attractive were not surprising—respondents see the Chinese market as providing many potential opportunities, largely as a function of the size of its internal market. The market is less attractive when one considers PRC government restrictions and economic and business practice differences.

Differences between U.S. respondents and Canadian respondents suggest that foreign investors may share some general concerns about the PRC but that different groups may also have different concerns. It is important that the PRC government be aware of these differences and consider tailoring its programs to these differing concerns. In the case of Canada and the United States, the PRC may want to offer U.S. investors guarantees regarding government interference, and Canadian investors assistance in understanding the differences in business practices. The differences identified are also of importance to home governments. Insofar as these governments wish to encourage their domestic companies to seek out opportunities in the PRC, they need to understand the concerns of these companies in order to encourage them effectively.

The implication of this research, for both U.S. and Canadian companies, is that the Chinese market is very attractive, but there are genuine concerns being voiced about doing business in the PRC. It is probably important for all business people considering doing business with the PRC to recognize that there are many fundamental differences between Chinese and North American management approaches; thus, it may be important to success to understand "the Chinese way." This can affect both exports to, and investment in, the PRC. Chinese culture was not considered important by these respondents, yet previous interviews (Punnett and He, 1988) suggested that living conditions in China are very hard for Westerners to accept, and that language can be a big problem. These previous interviews were with individuals who had spent considerable time in the PRC and it may be that respondents to the mail survey were less familiar with the reality of the PRC, and, therefore, more willing to dismiss the impact of Chinese culture on their ability to do business there.

This research sought to identify and assess some of the reasons why Canadians and Americans might differ in their approach to the PRC as well as to identify more generally how the two groups view opportunities in the PRC. A number of similarities as well as a number of differences between the two groups were identified. This gives some insight into how North American companies view the opportunities presented by the changing attitude of the PRC toward foreign business.

Understanding how the rest of the world views opportunities in the PRC is particularly important for the PRC government if it is to attract foreign investors successfully. This paper indicates the views of North American companies in 1988. Events in Beijing and other major cities in China during the summer of 1989 may have had an impact on the willingness of Westerners to do business in China. A current survey by one of the authors suggests that responses are mixed. Early responses to "Please describe your company's reactions to recent events in the People's Republic of China" range from "bad," through "wait and see," to "the recent events had no effect." The majority of respondents say that their plans for doing business in China have been slowed down. Clearly China continues to present a potentially very attractive market, but the events of the summer of 1989 serve to underscore the potential difficulties in accessing this market.

References

Beamish, P. (1984) "The Long March to China Trade." *Policy Options/Politiques*, pp. 30–33.

"China Issues New Rules Certifying Companies for Preferred Treatment." (1987) *Business Asia*, pp. 83.

Davidson, W. H. (1987) "Creating and Managing Joint Ventures in China." *California Management Review*, pp. 77–94.

"Foreign Funds Used in Wider Scope." (1985) *Beijing Review*, pp. 28, 29.

Grow, R. F. (1986) "Japanese and American Firms in China: Lessons of a New Market." *Columbia Journal of World Business*, pp. 49–56.

Hardin, H. (1974) *A Nation Unaware—The Canadian Economic Culture*. Vancouver: J. J. Douglas Ltd.

Hendryx, S. R. (1986) "The China Trade: Making the Deal Work." *Harvard Business Review*, 75, pp. 81–84.

Ho, P. S., and Huenemann, R. W. (1984) "China's Open Door Policy: The Quest for Foreign Technology and Capital." University of British Columbia.

Hofstede, G. (1981) *Culture's Consequences—International Differences in Work Related Values*. London: Sage Publications.

Jackofsky, E.; Slocum, J. W.; and McQuaid, S. J. (1988) "Cultural Values and the CEO: Alluring Companions?" *The Academy of Management Executive*. 11, pp. 39–49.

Lipsett, S. M. (1968) *Revolution and Counter-revolution*. New York: Basic Books.

National Accounts Statistics: Main Aggregates and Detailed Tables. (1987) New York: United Nations.

"New Chinese Rules State how Sino–Foreign Joint Ventures Can Solve Forex Problems." (1986) *Business Asia*, pp. 42–43.

"P.R.C. Strives to Revive Foreign Investor Interest with New Incentives Packages." (1986) *Business International*, pp. 339–340.

Punnett, B. J., and He, G. (1988) "The PRC—An Untapped Market Where Canadians Fear to Tread." *Canadian Business Review*, pp. 14–16.

Ruggles, R. L., Jr. (1983) "Environment for American Business Ventures in the People's Republic of China." *Columbia Journal of World Business*, pp. 67–73.

Rugman, A. M.; and McIllveen, J. (1985) *Megafirms*, Toronto: Methuen Publications.

Statistical Yearbook of the Republic of China. (1987) Directorate General of Budget, Accounting and Statistics, Executive Yuan, The Republic of China.

"The Big Fortune Cookies." (1986) *Canadian Business*, pp. 16–29.

"Time Ripe for Foreign Investment." (1987) *China Market*, pp. 6–8.

Tung, R. L. (1986) "Corporate Executives and Their Families in China: The Need for Cross-Cultural Understanding in Business." *Columbia Journal of World Business*, pp. 21–25.

Wang, N. T. (1986) "United States and China: Business Beyond Trade—An Overview." *Columbia Journal of World Business*, pp. 3–11.

Wei, J. (1985) "Legal Guarantees for Foreign Investors." *Beijing Review*.

"Who Will Be the Winner in China's Tech Import Market?" (1987) *China Market*, pp. 28–33.

Xu, R. (1985) "Rise of Purchasing Power in China." *China Market*, pp. 44–45.

Zamet, J. M., and Bovarnick, M. E. (1986) "Employee Relations for Multinational Companies in China." *Columbia Journal of World Business*, pp. 13–19.

HEIDI VERNON-WORTZEL, LAWRENCE H. WORTZEL,
AND ZHU JINGTIAN

The People's Republic of China as an Exporter

A Far Road Traveled, a Far Road yet to Go

Under Mao's leadership, the People's Republic of China (PRC) pursued an inward-looking development strategy based on self-reliance rather than on foreign technology, assistance, or capital equipment. With the adoption in the late 1970s of the economic development program, the Four Modernizations, China abruptly changed direction. Government placed a new emphasis on industrialization and exhibited a willingness to accept, even to search for, imported technology, capital equipment, and (when necessary) parts and components.

To pay for these imports, China had to generate a substantial increase in its foreign exchange earnings. Exports became a major source of the needed foreign exchange. In fact, enhanced exports were essential to the success of the Four Modernizations, because the program could not progress as rapidly as planned without the injection of imported capital goods, components, and other materials.

By either absolute or comparative standards, China has been extremely successful in increasing its exports, especially of manufactured goods. During the period from 1960 to 1978 China's exports increased at an average rate of 7.8 percent per year. From 1978 to 1985 exports grew at a rate of 15.7 percent per year. During the 1985–87 period, the growth rate spurted to 35 percent, and the proportion of manufactured goods increased from 33 to 50 percent. Although China's export growth during the 1978–87 period compared favorably with that of the South Asian Newly Industrialized Countries (NICs), its share of world exports was still minimal. For example, as of 1984, the East Asian NICs' share of world exports was 7.5 percent, while China's share amounted to just 1.3 percent (*Far Eastern Economic Review*, 1988; Krueger, 1986).

Most of China's exports of manufactures have been simple labor-intensive goods of low price and modest quality. China's returns from these exports have

Heidi Vernon-Wortzel is at Northeastern University, Boston. and Lawrence H. Wortzel is at Boston University; Zhu Jingtian is a graduate of Zhongshan University, PRC.

been quite small in relation to their final selling price. A substantial proportion were sold to Hong Kong middlemen, who then resold them in world markets, taking substantial markups in the process. Much of China's manufactured exports may have been sold at an economic loss, since in many cases the prices China obtained for the goods were less than their cost to produce.

Despite its outstanding export growth, China has experienced trade deficits since 1984. For its industrialization to continue, China must therefore increase its export earnings still further. China's export institutions have changed since 1978, as they responded to the demands of a more export-oriented government policy. But for growth to continue into the next decade, these organizations must undergo further changes in both their strategy and structure.

In this paper, we describe and analyze the structure of China's export institutions as they existed at the beginning of the export drive. We next describe and analyze the changes that have occurred through the 1980s, and recommend policies that will help China to continue to improve its performance in the 1990s. Our descriptions and analyses are based on published sources, on personal interviews with Chinese managers, and on interviews with foreign importers who have done business in China.

China is by no means a monolithic country. Differences abound among provinces and even among cities within the same province. It is a country of infinite complexity, and one in which changes happen rapidly and not always in a linear direction. Our examples come primarily from Guangdong province in the south of China and from its major city, Guangzhou (Canton). This area of the country is a bellwether of change and has led China's export drive; however institutions in Guangdong are not identical in structure or strategy to those in every other province or city.

The structure of China's export institutions before 1979

During the 1949–78 period, China preferred to satisfy its domestic needs with domestically produced goods; exports were only to generate enough income to compensate for shortfalls in local production. Each year, the Beijing government determined export targets based on estimated foreign exchange needs. Beijing then allocated the targets among twelve state-level foreign trade corporations (FTCs), each of which had a monopoly on a specific list of export products. The FTCs, in turn, distributed their targets among their provincial- and municipal-level subsidiary corporations. All control, however, remained in Beijing. A provincial subsidiary corporation could not export without the permission of its Beijing parent (Vernon-Wortzel, 1983).

Except for some activity at trade fairs, the FTCs did virtually no marketing. Instead, they waited for customers actively seeking Chinese merchandise to find them. Buyers did come, principally seeking lower prices than could be obtained elsewhere. These buyers had to do business with the FTCs, since the

FTCs interjected themselves between their foreign customers and the producing factories. Although buyers were allowed to visit factories to assess their production capabilities, they rarely negotiated directly with factory managers for price, quantity, or other elements of a contract. The buyer negotiated with the FTC, which then made production arrangements with a factory.

The system in place prior to the introduction of the Four Modernizations in 1977 may have adequately served China's needs at that time. It required minimal diversion of either time or effort from the products the factories were producing for local consumption. The system also insulated the local producers from what the government considered the contamination of foreign influence. Tight control from Beijing ensured that domestic production goals would still be met; factories were not tempted by the prospect of earning foreign exchange, since all foreign exchange earnings remained with the central government. The producing factories' role in the export process was simply as passive suppliers to the FTCs.

There was, therefore, little incentive for producers to export, let alone to expand exports. Moreover, the inwardly focused and cumbersome system mitigated against developing all but the simplest new products or expanding production of goods already being made for the domestic market. Yet the experience of the successful South Asian exporters demonstrates the importance of direct communication and coordination between producer and customer in developing extensive export businesses (Wortzel and Vernon-Wortzel, 1981). The FTCs, of course, made such direct contact virtually impossible.

The FTCs had no more incentive to expand their exports than did the producers. Many were running at an economic loss. In order to get any business at all, they often had to sell their exports at prices below the domestic price they were required to pay the producing factory. Having contacts with foreigners was much frowned upon by those in power. The FTCs could work with foreign buyers who sought them out, but FTC employees who actively pursued foreign buyers might find themselves criticized for such activity. The organization culture of the FTCs, in common with the culture of other organizations in the PRC at the time, was xenophobic, bureaucratic, and anti-entrepreneurial (Laaksonen, 1984).

Organizing to expand foreign trade:
the first changes

After 1978, the new emphasis on exports gave rise to profound changes in China's foreign trading system. One major change was the creation of Special Economic Zones (SEZs) dedicated to manufacturing only for export. However, manufacturing firms in the SEZs have so far accounted for a small proportion of China's exports; the bulk of its exports have been products manufactured within the domestic market and sold through the FTCs. Exports from the SEZs may well skyrocket in the 1990s, however.

As economic reform proceeded, China's state-owned companies were expected to stand on their own and compete with other state, collective, private, and foreign firms on the basis of price and quality of services. Manufacturing firms became more and more free to choose what they would produce and to whom they would sell (*China Business Review*, 1984). Relationships between the provincial FTCs and the central government FTCs and between the FTCs and producing companies changed. Under the economic reforms, some of the provincial FTCs began to operate as independent units, making their own deals rather than taking direction from Beijing. Some of the larger factories could even negotiate directly with prospective customers.

Adaptation to change

The FTCs tried to respond to their new and expanded role. Both the internal organization of the FTCs and the Chinese organization culture made the task difficult. Typically, an FTC was a combination of product and functional organization. The selling side, or sales section, of the organization was organized by broad product groups, while all of the necessary support functions (e.g., accounting, procurement of packaging material, and shipping) were organized centrally and served all product groups. An FTC might have as many as a dozen product groups in its sales section.

The people in the sales section served as both an inside and outside sales force. Their principal outside sales activity was traveling to various parts of the world to participate in trade fairs and shows. But they spent the bulk of their time on inside sales, working with customers who came to see them in China. The people in the sales section were the link between customer and producer. They took orders from customers and passed the orders on to whichever factories they considered appropriate.

In accepting and filling an order, the sales section had to work with several other sections in the FTC, which were organized by function: an import section to import any parts unavailable locally; a packaging section to decide on and procure packaging material; a shipping and transportation section to warehouse and transport finished goods from the factory, and to prepare all the required export documents and arrange for shipping; and a vehicle team to transport the goods.

In addition, a planning section set quotas and limits on the sales section's activities. It worked with the government, for example, to limit exports of goods that were in short supply and to encourage exports of goods in surplus. A trade development section was responsible for developing exports of previously unexported products, while a commercial information section passed on information about government export policy toward various countries, as well as demand and price levels in countries of interest. An administrative section included a foreign affairs office that received foreign visitors and arranged foreign travel for FTC employees. It also provided clerical, typing, and photocopying services to the entire FTC.

How the system worked: the effects of change

The FTCs worked best in handling transactions for items that factories were already producing, which did not require changes in either product or packaging for export, and which were not in great demand domestically. When modifications were required in order to make an export sale, the internal workings of the FTCs and their changing relationships with the factories made export transactions extremely cumbersome.

To make a packaging change requested by a customer, for example, the sales section would have to work with the packaging section to implement the change. In the case of product changes, the FTC would have to interpret the changes for the producing factory and then enter into extensive negotiations with the factory in order to get the factory to produce what the would-be buyer wanted. There were few incentives for factories to modify products for export.

Moreover, the culture of Chinese organizations still mitigated against working with foreigners. In most cases, although salespeople did make periodic trips abroad, they did not actively prospect for customers. The FTCs' foreign sales were still confined principally to firms and individuals who actively sought them out. Much of China's foreign trade continued to go through Hong Kong middlemen, who searched China for lower-cost sources of merchandise that had become too expensive to produce in Hong Kong.

Chinese organization culture did not encourage open, cooperative relationships within the FTC nor between FTCs and producers. In the Chinese organization, information still is power and a source of personal advantage to its possessor. Therefore, information was a commodity to be hoarded and doled out as sparingly as possible. Loosening the reins from Beijing increased the amount of proprietary information. Hence, information became even more valuable to its holder.

While the Four Modernizations gave both the FTCs and the factories the freedom to export, it also gave them the freedom not to. In many cases, factories' priorities favored domestic sales rather than exports. Domestic demand, especially for consumer goods, was burgeoning and many items were in short supply. Factories had incentives to sell domestically, but there were no incentives to export. Factories could not keep the foreign exchange earned from exports; moreover, their export price had to be the same as their domestic price.

If the FTC handling the sale obtained an export price higher than the domestic price, it kept the difference (plus the foreign exchange resulting from the sale). The producing factory gained no *guanxi* (influence) from exporting. But, if it sold domestically, it could trade or direct some of its output for needed raw materials, capital equipment, or favors.

In some cases, though, an FTC could encourage exports where none would otherwise take place. It could use its foreign exchange to purchase needed capital goods for a cooperative factory. It could also subsidize exports. In numerous instances, a product's domestic price exceeded the price at which it could be exported. In such instances, the FTC would absorb the difference between the domestic and export price, allowing the factory to realize the domestic price for its exports.

The system worked best for products not in short supply in China and which required at most a bare minimum of modification for export markets. It also favored the export of standardized, staple products for which an importer could tolerate long lead times between placing and receiving an order. The system offered little incentive for producers to increase their productivity and little opportunity for them to learn how to better manufacture to the requirements of export markets. The FTCs continued to insulate producers both from the economic realities of export prices and from contact with customers from whom they could learn.

For the most part, therefore, China's exports of manufactures consisted of simple, easy-to-produce, labor-intensive products at the bottom end of the price/quality spectrum in their category. With the exception of products such as specialized handicraft items, all China had to offer a buyer was low price. In many cases, these low prices were made possible by extremely low wage rates coupled with the willingness of the FTCs to export even at an economic loss.

For several reasons, including lack of worker incentives, uncertain raw materials supplies, and poor understanding of buyers' requirements, China's factories were simply not efficient or reliable producers. Indeed, China's success as an exporter has been due much more to the persistence of foreign importers actively searching for merchandise than to Chinese sellers actively looking for customers. In this regard, however, China's role has been little different from that of the Four Tigers in their early exporting years. But importing from China required, in addition, much patience and persistence.

The active role played by the Hong Kong traders was a mixed blessing for the PRC. Because of the FTCs' limited direct contacts with overseas markets, the Hong Kong traders played a necessary role in marketing China's exports. China's exports would surely have been considerably smaller without its Hong Kong connection, but the Hong Kong middlemen also inhibited both producers' and FTCs' contact with overseas buyers, while at the same time taking substantial markups for their services. The Hong Kong traders had a vested interest in keeping producers and overseas buyers apart.

Recent changes in the system and their effects

Recognizing the inadequacies in the system, the Chinese government, during the late 1980s, instituted changes it believed would further expand exports. These changes were designed to further loosen the relationship between the FTCs and the producing factories, and to provide the factories with better incentives to export.

The government gave some of its leading factories the right to export directly, without involving the FTCs in negotiations. In addition, it allowed such factories to retain at least a portion of the foreign exchange they earned through exporting. This change came at a time when factories were becoming responsible for profits and losses. Factories were no longer guaranteed customers and had to pay close attention to quality, delivery, and finding reliable suppliers. They had much more leeway in branching out into new and more profitable product lines. With permission to keep some of the foreign exchange they earned, factories had a stronger motivation to export. They could use the foreign exchange they earned to import the capital equipment required for modernization and expansion.

However, the right to export directly did not free the factories from the FTCs; in many cases, FTCs still performed a service role, arranging for shipping and handling the required extensive paperwork. In addition, the factories still used the FTCs as conduits for their imports of capital equipment.

So far, the right to export directly has been of little value to factories. Most have had very limited success in attracting customers. The government wants its factory managers to be entrepreneurs. But these managers find it difficult to get access to information about export opportunities, to buy appropriate machinery, and to hire workers with the necessary skills. The factories that have benefited most have been those that were already significant exporters. They knew what to produce and had customers in hand; they could therefore bypass the FTCs without too much difficulty. The threat of losing their leading factories is making the FTCs, in turn, more entrepreneurial, albeit very slowly.

Quite probably, the most entrepreneurial exporting organizations since 1978 have been those in the SEZs. As an incentive to manufacture for export, the SEZs were allowed to keep 100 percent of the foreign exchange they earned. The idea, of course, was that the SEZ manufacturers would then import components and capital equipment to expand their manufacturing capacity. What has happened, however, is that some SEZ firms have been functioning as trading companies rather than manufacturing companies. As an incentive to turn in their foreign-exchange earnings, firms in the SEZ have been allowed to buy domestic currency (renminbi) at two times the official exchange rate. They have been using this privilege to buy domestically produced goods from factories in other provinces in China. They then export those goods at lower prices than the producers charge" (Cheng, 1989).

Evaluating the changes before Tiananmen

The environment for manufactured exports from the industrializing countries has become increasingly competitive during the 1980s, and will be even more competitive in the coming decade. For many of the products the industrializing countries export, demand is growing slowly, while the number of producing countries (and firms within them) is increasing faster than demand. Erstwhile suppliers will have to fight harder and harder for the attention of buyers, then offer lower prices, better quality, and faster delivery to keep customers (Vernon-Wortzel, Wortzel, and Deng, 1988).

While China's exports have increased monumentally since instituting the Four Modernizations, paradoxically Chinese producers have not become more competitive suppliers. Many, if not most, have neither become significantly more efficient nor have they significantly upgraded the quality of their products. Some have even become less competitive. In more and more cases, China is no longer the low-cost producer. Interviews with U.S. importers established that Chinese exporters' prices for products as diverse as chemicals, rubber gloves, and electric fans are no longer competitive. Inflation has made locally produced raw materials and components more expensive, and has put pressure on wages. Devaluations have made imported materials and equipment more expensive. Factories are under pressure to earn profits or, at least, not to incur losses. And the FTCs are being discouraged from absorbing losses in cases where the export price must be lower than the domestic prices.

Burgeoning domestic demand for consumer goods and for the raw materials required to produce them competes with export demand. The domestic market is easier to satisfy than the export market, because domestic buyers will often accept lower-quality goods. And Chinese managers, even those involved in exporting, seem to lack an understanding of foreign buyers. They do not fully understand buyers' requirements for uniform quality and on-time delivery of the full quantity of merchandise that is ordered. Moreover, xenophobia and bureaucracy still characterize many Chinese organizations. Importing from China remains a demanding task, and, given an alternative, many buyers prefer to search elsewhere first.

At the same time, China is developing some world-class producers, eager to export and capable of doing so. Invariably, these are firms that have had close and continuous contact with foreign buyers, principally through contract manufacturing. In such cases, the contractor has been able to supervise, control, and teach its contracts how to improve quality and efficiency. China's tasks are to increase the number of eager and capable exporters and to make it easier for foreign buyers to do business with them.

Recommendations

Prospective foreign buyers must have easier access to potential producers. Studies of importers' criteria for choosing suppliers indicate that the ability to have direct contact with the producer is a significant determinant of supplier choice (Deng and Wortzel, 1989). Moreover, direct contact with buyers is the key to upgrading the capabilities of Chinese producers. The history of the successful exporters based in industrializing countries is that they learned from their customers.

Providing incentives for the factories to export is also important. Studies of exporter behavior indicate that the strongest deterrent to exporting is a large and growing home market (Bilkey, 1978). During the last ten years, China's domestic market has certainly fit that description. Even where the home market has been less of a deterrent (in South Korea, for example), the government had to offer significant incentives in order for its firms to export (Rhee, 1985). Export business is much more difficult and much riskier than domestic business; without sufficient incentives, firms simply will not bother. If China continues its progress toward a market-driven economy, export incentives will become even more important. In the increasing absence of government directives, firms will be more and more driven by economic considerations, which will often favor the domestic market over exports. China's exporters must become considerably more aggressive in searching for and attracting buyers. The history of the Four Tigers (the successful Asian NIC exporters: South Korea, Taiwan, Hong Kong, and Singapore) is that much of their export business started as the result of importer pull from buyers located in the United States and Europe who sought them out (Hone, 1974). At the time, these buyers had no sources of merchandise other than their own domestic suppliers, and the Four Tigers' firms had to compete only against higher-cost suppliers located in the importers' countries. Now, the competitive focus has changed, and an erstwhile Chinese exporter must compete for the business not just against the Four Tigers but also against countries such as India, Indonesia, Thailand, and Sri Lanka. The Four Tigers' experience indicates that it is the factories, not the FTCs, that should take the active lead role in marketing China's exports. And the factories cannot do the marketing adequately from within China. They must make contact with buyers in the buyers' home countries, rather than waiting for them to come to China. Because of intense competition, sellers can no longer wait for buyers to seek them out.

But, at least for the near term, encouraging the FTCs to continue in a service role is extremely important. The factories do not yet have the expertise to manage the paperwork and shipping involved in export transactions. Lessons learned from the Japanese *Sogo Shosha* suggest, moreover, that the FTCs can play an active role in marketing commodity products, such as bulk chemicals and certain fabrics.

Unfortunately, marketing alone will not be enough to keep China's exports growing. Despite a few world-class plants, China has serious problems on the manufacturing side in meeting production schedules, in quality control, and in cost control. There is a great deal still to learn, and an acute shortage of teachers to guide the learning. Without an infusion of experienced Chinese-speaking manufacturing engineers, the needed learning will be slow and difficult.

Even before the student demonstrations in June 1989, the Chinese government exhibited a growing concern with internal economic problems, such as the rampant inflation, a growing gap in wealth among regions and across professions, large-scale unemployment, and mass migration to the cities. All of these problems jeopardized the efforts of FTCs to export quality goods at realistic prices.

After the events in May and June, culminating in the Tiananmen Square Massacre, the Chinese government did an abrupt political "about-face." Although the central government in Beijing issues periodic assurances of continued support for exports and foreign investment, political actions suggest otherwise. The affluent areas along the coast and in southern China are increasingly under attack as hot spots of "bourgeois liberalism." Capitalism and profit motivation are no longer held in high esteem. Foreign managers who left in June have been slow to return.

The Chinese government is sending fewer and fewer students abroad to study. Students within China spend a year in the army for political indoctrination rather than in the classroom for technical training. Students and managers are reluctant to speak to Westerners and to gather information about foreign markets. More than any other single factor, the anti-Western rhetoric and hard line on Chinese–foreign interaction imperils the progress FTCs have made in developing export markets. Access to information is critical if progress is to continue. Unhappily, ideology and an export-oriented economy are now at odds in China.

References

Bilkey, Warren J. (1978) "An Attempted Integration of the Literature on the Export Behavior of Firms." *Journal of International Business Studies*, Spring/Summer, pp. 33–46.

Cheng, Elizabeth. (1989) "Beggar Thy Neighbor." *Far Eastern Economic Review*, 12 January, pp. 45–46.

The China Business Review. (1984) September/October, p. 4.

Deng, Sheng Liang, and Wortzel, Lawrence H. (1989) U.S. Importers' Supply Selection Criteria and Information Source Use. Working Paper, Boston University School of Management, Boston, MA.

Far Eastern Economic Review. (1988) "Managing China's Open Door." 17 November, pp. 89–90.

Hone, Angus. (1974) "Multinational Corporations and Multinational Buying Groups: Their Impact on the Growth of Asia's Exports of Manufactures—Myths and Realities." *World Development*, February, pp. 145–149.

Krueger, A. O. 1986 "The Effects of Trade Strategies on Growth." *Finance and Development*, June 1986, pp. 51–59.

Laaksonen, Oliva. (1984) "The Management and Power Structure of Chinese Enterprises during and after the Cultural Revolution; with Empirical Data Comparing Chinese and European Enterprises." *Organization Studies*, 5 (1), pp. 1–21.

Rhee, Young W. (1985) *Instruments for Export Policy and Administration.* World Bank Staff Working Paper, No. 725, Washington, D.C.

Vernon-Wortzel, Heidi. (1983) "Equity and Efficiency in the Distribution of Non-Food Consumer Goods in China." *Asian Survey*, Summer, pp. 845–853.

Vernon-Wortzel, Heidi, and Wortzel, Lawrence H. (1987) "Manufactured Exports from the Developing Counties." In George Westacott, ed., *Managing in a Global Economy*. Eastern Academy of Management and Deree College, Athens, Greece, pp. 203–207.

Vernon-Wortzel, Heidi; Wortzel, Lawrence H.; and Deng, Sheng Liang. (1988) "Do Neophyte Exporters Understand Importers? U.S. Importers' Decision Criteria and PRC Exporters' Perceptions about Supplier Selection and Information Source Use." *Columbia Journal of World Business*, Winter, pp. 49–56.
Wortzel, Lawrence H., and Vernon-Wortzel, Heidi. (1981) "Export Marketing Strategies for NIC and LDC-Based Firms." *Columbia Journal of World Business*, Spring, pp. 51–60.

Index

About the Editor

Oded Shenkar received a B.A. degree in both East-Asian studies and sociology as well as an MSc.soc. in sociology from the Hebrew University of Jerusalem. He later received M.Phil and Ph.D. degrees from Columbia University, where he wrote his dissertation on the Chinese bureaucracy. Since 1982, he has been with the Leon Recanati Graduate School of Business Administration at Tel-Aviv University, where he is now a Senior Lecturer. Dr. Shenkar is also affiliated with the University of Hawaii. He has written articles on Chinese comparative management, which have appeared in noted management journals.